Life

at the Speed of

Passion

Life

at the Speed of

Passion

Create a Life of Intention, Purpose, and Integrity

EVE WRIGHT, ESQ.

CAREER
PRESS
Pompton Plains, N.J.

LIFE AT THE SPEED OF PASSION
EDITED AND TYPESET BY KARA KUMPEL
Cover design by Joanna Williams
Printed in the U.S.A.

To order this title, please call toll-free 1-800-CAREER-1 (NJ and Canada: 201-848-0310) to order using VISA or MasterCard, or for further infor-mation on books from Career Press.

The Career Press, Inc.
220 West Parkway, Unit 12
Pompton Plains, NJ 07444
www.careerpress.com

Library of Congress Cataloging-in-Publication Data
Wright, Eve.
    Life at the speed of passion : create a life of intention, purpose, and integrity / by Eve Wright, Esq.
        pages cm
    Includes index.
    ISBN 978-1-60163-314-9 -- ISBN 978-1-60163-472-6 (ebook) 1. Self-actualization (Psychology) 2. Self-realization. 3. Interest (Psychology) 4. Job satisfaction. 5. Satisfaction. 6. Success. I. Title.

BF637.S4W725 2014
158.1--dc23
                                                                2014000406

Acknowledgments

To my daughter, whose focus, persistence, and independent streak are reminiscent of her mother's.

To my mother and my husband, thank you for your unwavering love and support of me and my relentless pursuit of the infinite possibilities.

To my work family (particularly "the gals"), the friends I interviewed, and those to whom I refer in admiration in this book, thank you for your humor, your candor, your life lessons, and your infinite ability to inspire.

Contents

Chapter 1

How to Create the Spark You Need for a Passion-Filled Life

Do you have a philosophy that shapes your life? I do. As a matter of fact, these days I never leave home without it. It is quite a simple one, actually:

There is nothing I cannot achieve.

Maybe it doesn't sound that simple, but trust me, you will find that it is once you start living it for yourself. This philosophy is the driving force of my belief system, and it compels me to strive for excellence each and every day. Pursuing goals, both personal and professional, is key to my success. But this was not always so.

When I was younger, I had a tendency to focus on my academic career. I pursued my academic goals with zeal, but in my personal life, I lagged behind. As I matured, I realized why my personal life was not very satisfying: I was not constructing the same framework for my personal success and happiness as I was for my academic pursuits. I realized that if I wanted to achieve the same level of success with my personal life, changes needed to be made. So I went to work on creating a framework that would help me achieve both professional and personal success.

My first step was to explore interests and activities outside of my studies. Once I started looking, I gleefully discovered a world of interests that could consume and fulfill me just as much as my academic career had, and I realized that my personal triumphs could be just as remarkable as those of my academic career. My mother used to say to me, "There is no need to waste a perfectly good life waiting on moments that never come." Her wise words did not resonate with me fully until I was mature enough to see the wisdom in her philosophy. This was her way of telling me to think outside the box and unearth my true potential to achieve my greatest success. Now, I am passing that advice on to you: Never let yourself be defined by another person's expectations. Continually reject the labels people want to force on you. Once I broke free from the labels and boundaries set for me, I was able to unlock my full potential. My ability to set my own agenda and embrace my passions with abandon allowed me to see far beyond my own imagination.

Shattering Your Own Personal Expectation Ceiling

I believe we all suffer from a personal expectation ceiling. Now, you may have heard of glass ceilings before—the invisible barriers many women feel inhibit them from climbing up the corporate ladder—but we can also set our own ceiling made of our personal expectations of what we are able to achieve. These ceilings are often formed from and influenced by fears about stepping outside and exploring new challenges. Our goal is to recognize these limitations and shatter this ceiling by raising the bar and challenging ourselves to excel beyond the paths that have been chosen for us.

This is possible because we are all in charge of our own destiny. I am here to tell you that there is no room in your life for negativity and defeatist attitudes that drag you down. You can become so bogged down with negative thoughts and a "woe is me" attitude that you simply fail to achieve. Never allow other people and their "expectation ceiling"—nor even the one you make yourself—to define what you are capable of achieving. You are the captain of your ship and solely responsible for your happiness and success. The right attitude will propel you forward and allow you to shake free of the chains of others' notions that attempt to define you. You are limitless. Your ability to succeed depends on your belief in yourself and your ideas.

Here's an example from my life that illustrates how breaking free of others' expectations and the roles they have assigned to you is the best move you can make. When I was in law school, I wanted a particular law clerk position, but the people around me were intent on talking me out of it, pointing out how it would require me to pick up and move to a strange city where I would be all alone, and how the position wouldn't count toward my law school program. "Why would you want to go there and do that? Why uproot your whole life when things are fine where you are?" These were the questions I received when I talked about my plans to conquer the challenge. But I was not deterred, and I harassed (in a nice way) the hell out of a group of individuals until I got the position. Then I dug in and convinced my school to give me credit for the clerkship. And my challenge did not stop there. I also found a way, by hook and by crook, to secure a temporary place to live and a job to cover my expenses. Soon I was making my way in a new city all by myself, and it was one of the best things I could have done.

That's just one example of how other people and their negative, defeatist attitudes can try to shape your life. I could have taken their advice to heart and followed the traditional path—it certainly would have been easier.

But, honestly, all the effort I put forth to achieve my goal was so worth it. I am here to tell you that once you start to figure out the life you want for yourself and then work to make it your reality, the world opens up! It is almost as though the expectation ceilings, defeatist attitudes, and negativity are dark clouds in your life that are burned away by the sunshine that is you.

Initiating Change: *Two Paths Diverged in the Woods, and I Took the One Less Traveled*

This same philosophy—that there is nothing you can't achieve—also applies to your personal life. I grew up in the Midwest state of Indiana, and my upbringing there instilled in me a strong sense of resistance to a "woe is me" attitude. I truly have little patience for pity parties, so please do not send me an invitation to one. I believe strongly in the idea that when you're faced with setbacks you need to brush yourself off and get on with it. If you are not going to change direction and improve your attitude or outlook when roadblocks form, then you are destined to fail. I wholeheartedly embrace the notion that, as long as we have a breath in our body, we have an opportunity to change our lives.

This is not to say that we don't all get into a funk sometimes and need some time to just shut the door and lick our wounds. We all need to escape every now and then. The problem comes when this develops into a daily habit and becomes part of your personality. I can tell you that achieving greatness is difficult, but it's nearly impossible when the bulk of your energy is used up by your perpetually holding up the wall at the pity party. That kind of mentality is toxic: it magnifies your insecurities, reinforces your self-doubt, and undermines belief in your ability to realize the life you want to live.

Enter the spark. The spark is the moment that changes everything, if you let it. It is about awareness and willingness, and being open to the potential opportunities that result from the discovery of your true passion(s). Once you open your mind to discovering new hobbies and interests, your individual spark will grow into a flame.

It may take courage and boldness to pursue them, but opportunities to expand and think outside of your comfort zone are all around you. New experiences and adventures can be discovered at every turn. You only need to be courageous and open to exciting events that can—and will—expand your horizons and help you find your true passion. Here's an example: I am not particularly fond of cold weather, but when I moved to Minnesota, I ended up meeting groups of people who loved to ski. The next thing I knew, I was joining a ski club, attending ski conferences, and, in general, having a blast. I would never have believed a girl who hates the cold as much as I do would be swooshing down the slopes having the time of her life. Am I ever going to be an

Olympic skier? No, but that is not the point. The point is that I opened myself up to a new experience and found my spark. And you can too, if you believe in yourself and look for a spark that can develop into a flame, which will ultimately create the fire in your life!

This can happen on a personal level, and it can even impact you on a professional basis. Igniting your passion requires equal measures of three ingredients: art, science, and common sense.

1. **Art:** Use your imagination and creativity to brainstorm ideas. You can unleash your potential with the power of insight and forethought. The potential to discover something you love is at your fingertips. The art and grace of positive thinking and the avoidance of negative thoughts can propel you and ignite an ember that is difficult to extinguish.

2. **Science:** With scientific principles, you can quantify and see measurable results after igniting your passion. You can set goals for yourself and watch as you achieve each step. Having a set of specific rules and guidelines can spark this passion and deliver results that are tangible.

3. **Common sense:** The same can be said with your innate common sense. It will direct you to pursue interests you love and expand on these interests with the guiding principles of discipline, interest, enthusiasm, and a drive to succeed at a level you never thought possible.

Type-A Personalities: Why We Tend to be Unfulfilled

For some of us, getting that spark started is challenging because we let the best—and worst—of us get in the way. Everybody knows the Type-A personality stereotype: a hard-driving individual who is obsessed with perfection and drives himself and the people around him to excellence—and sometimes madness. I tend to shy away from generalizations, preferring to focus on individuals rather than labels, but I can apply this stereotype to my own personality and others I have known to form a checklist of traits we share.

Does this sound like you?

* Ambitious
* Assertive
* Competitive
* High-achiever
* Somewhat aggressive
* Sometimes controlling
* Preoccupied with status
* Sometimes highly strung

Each of these characteristics has applied to me, in varying degrees, throughout my life. At times, each trait has been dominant. The point of identifying each trait is to use it for greater fulfillment instead of letting it control your life.

The main reason I believe some Type-A personalities are not fulfilled is because they are progressing in a role based on hierarchy and societal expectations. Your families, your school, your church, your sorority, and your social club all build the framework in which you operate, and these external forces drive you. Unfortunately, this does not allow for personal growth and exploration. You are placed in a mold that has been defined by other peoples' expectations of you, and this has not allowed you to express your own individuality.

Oftentimes, we are boxed in by social sets and familial obligations, and we live in a world not of our own making. We have hobbies and activities defined by these social pressures that may not necessarily be our interests. Our job is to recognize this and push the boundaries to discover our own individuality. Otherwise, we are left unfulfilled and unhappy with our situation. The good news is that you can change this by sparking a new course for yourself.

Redefining Yourself Every Day:
What It Means to Be Happy

As we grow and mature, our lives change, and we re-assess what it means to "have it all." I know my priorities have changed throughout the years, as has my outlook, and I expect to reflect back in 10 years and see more significant changes to my viewpoint. This is growth, and it is good. Your perspective of life shifts as you grow with experience and maturity.

So, let us look at what defines "having it all." For some people this might mean a high-octane career, a high-achieving spouse who looks like a supermodel, two freshly scrubbed super-children, and a multi-million-dollar mansion that was decorated by the "right" decorator. However, I think the notion of "having it all" should be defined much differently. Having it all is not about material possessions and the right accessories; it's about enjoying the freedom to pursue your life goals and connect with your loved ones. Having it all also includes having your health. I cannot stress this enough. And, speaking of stress, it will affect your life and health in ways you have never imagined. Stress cripples. It is as simple as that. Stress will destroy your physical health, your emotional well-being, and your mental outlook. The key is to develop strategies to minimize stress and mold a better-rounded you. People who achieve a balanced life can give and receive love better.

Another key to "having it all" is indeed financial freedom. Along with mental and physical freedom it forms a triad that allows you to become the happiest possible version of yourself.

Our Own Version of Success:
Channeling Your Potential

I am frequently asked how I define and experience success. This is an easy question, and I have my mother to thank for the answer. I define and experience success through blowing the doors off of the goals I pursue, which, to me, means doing my best each and every time. It is as simple as that.

When I was a child, my mother and I used to have battle royales about grades. I had always done well academically, but there was always a little voice in the back of my head challenging me to do better. Okay, maybe it was not a little voice; it was a big voice, and it belonged to my mother. She continually challenged me to excel. If I brought home an A-minus, then she would ask me why it was not an A. This offended me. I was at the top of my class, so I could not figure out for the life of me why she was riding me about an A-minus. I later realized that her criticism was not about the grade. It had to do with the effort I had put into receiving it. What she was really asking was, "Is this your best work, and did you study as hard as possible?"

It took me some time to figure out where she was coming from, but, once I realized it, I could see her point. There is no reason to attempt something unless you are going to give it your best effort. This doesn't mean I have to excel at every endeavor. It simply means I must put forth the energy and focus to give 100 percent each time I attempt to do something.

Where's Your Flint? *You Have a Spark to Make*

Results do not come all by themselves. Some action or event must set things in motion to produce results. Think of this as the spark I talked about earlier. It's what creates the heat to light the flames that ignite the passion in your life. To spark, we have to use the right materials and we also must be engaged in the process.

When I was looking to add stories to this book beyond my own sparks, I looked to my colleagues and friends who have inspired me. They're not celebrities, but hopefully they will be people you can relate to. After all, the spark is not about fame or fortune; it is about you and what pushes you to make those significant, and very necessary, changes in your life.

Meet *Carmen Wong*

The inspirations that ignite the spark are different from person to person. For Carmen Wong, there was no one pivotal moment. Rather, she experienced a string of "aha!" moments when the lightbulb came on and she was driven to action.

Carmen was part of the first generation in her family to have access to advanced education. Although she knew this was important, it also created pressure for her to move in directions that she did not want to go. For example, to make her mother happy, Carmen started her undergraduate work as a pre-med major. She took one organic chemistry class before she went to her administrator and said that this was not for her. At the time, her mother was very disappointed with Carmen's subsequent choice of an art history and psychology degree. (Carmen did eventually win her mother's approval when she went to work for Christie's Auction House on Park Avenue.)

Conversely, Carmen saw her mom as an unhappy and unfulfilled woman who was not doing what she wanted to do, but rather went with what she thought the Dominican society in which she was raised expected of her. The years went by as she played her traditional role, never realizing her full potential.

When Carmen's mother passed away at the young age of 59, Carmen was hit with the realization that life is incredibly short. Still, she maintained the status quo and went to work every day at Time, Inc.'s *Money Magazine*, where she was an editor as well as a member of the executive diversity committee and the African-American & Asian group, and co-chair of the Hispanic Affinity Group. She lived and breathed the Time, Inc. culture; it had become her identity and all that she knew. She was a hard-working, faithful, and dedicated employee, but she felt underutilized. Everywhere she looked she saw ceilings and barriers that left her feeling unfulfilled. She kept hoping that her job would eventually lead to happiness, but as she climbed the corporate ladder, it dawned on her that happiness was *not* waiting around the corner.

Carmen had spent so much time trying to make her mother proud and happy that it took a life-changing circumstance for her to realize it was okay to start thinking about herself and what would make *her* happy. This spark lit for Carmen just months after losing her mother, when a new editor-in-chief came in to *Money Magazine* with his own people and let everyone else—including Carmen—go. This was the "aha!" moment. She now had an opportunity— in fact, almost a requirement—to figure out what would make her happy. It took losing her job to convince Carmen to take a chance.

Here she was, with no job and no money coming in, yet all she could think about was how short life was and how she needed to make herself happy. It was almost as soon as she made this decision to change her life that great things started to happen for her.

While Carmen was at *Money Magazine*, she had realized that there were not many people like herself who knew how to manage their finances—which was why readership was so high at the magazine. Carmen could see that people were searching for more knowledge on the subject, particularly from people who really lived, worked, and breathed finance. It was an untapped area that Carmen saw as an opportunity to help people the way she had always wanted to—not through medicine, as she had first thought, but through helping people manage their money.

Now, after her layoff, this became the impetus she needed to become her own boss in the world of freelance writing: She decided to use the expertise she had gained through her job at *Money Magazine* to write a book for young people on the importance of successfully managing their money. That book became *Generation Debt: Take Control of Your Money—A How-to Guide* (New York: Grand Central Publishing, 2006), which has been featured on the recommended reading list of *The Wall Street Journal.*

Soon after writing *Generation Debt*, things started falling into place for Carmen. Within a year of her book being published, she had three television offers. Carmen now believes that when you go toward what you should be doing, which is being fulfilled, good things come to you. She does issue a word of warning here, though: people should not just go out and say, "I love to dance, therefore I will quit my job and dance." There still has to be strategy for what to do once the spark ignites—you need to have a plan for how you can turn your love of dance into a career that puts food on the table.

Carmen, for instance, went with something she knew, and did not necessarily make a 180-degree life change. She entered a career niche she was familiar with and worked toward making it into what she enjoyed and what she wanted to do with her life. She had just been doing it in the wrong environment previously; now she had the freedom to control what she was doing, and could determine who she was as a worker and as a person.

Carmen understands how this type of change can pose a real risk to stability. When she started out on her freelance pathway (sparked by the loss of her job), she was pregnant, she and her then-husband had a mortgage, and they only had $500 in the bank. Along the way she experienced plenty of breakdown moments when she wondered what she was doing. But she continued to follow her spark, and soon enough the checks started coming in.

Now, as a single mom, she looks at the choices she's faced with in terms of whether they will provide real fulfillment. For example, she has had some opportunities to go back to television full-time, but has turned them down because she feels it is important to control her schedule so that she can make her daughter her number-one priority.

Carmen offers this advice to overcome the pressure many people feel to go with the status quo and what family and society says we should be doing: "I think many of us want to be successful and be stable, but we have to figure out what that looks like. What do *we* want it to look like? Is it really about wanting to be able to buy the car? Or is it about something else?"

There's a saying she heard somewhere that she now tells herself every day: "The pressure is a privilege." Whenever she hears someone complaining that he has so much work or that he is so busy, her response is, "What is the alternative?" It's all about perspective, really. Nothing really works if you're in a state of resentment; if you feel that way, then it is probably your internal voice telling you that something is not right. And that could just be the spark that needs to be acted on!

A wise man once said, "Know thyself." This is at the heart of igniting your spark, because you must find a spark that is true to who you are, or it won't catch fire. Once you know yourself, then Carmen believes you can move forward in a positive, strong way. Knowing yourself is not a once-and-done endeavor, though. It is a continual process, because what defines happiness and fulfillment for you will change as time goes on, and so the things that spark you will have to change as well. The spark will evolve as you do.

Parting Words

As I have grown, I have adjusted my approach to life, prioritizing and devoting my energies to pursuits that interest me. I define and experience success by taking the time in both my personal and professional life to enjoy the journey as well as arriving at the destination. And I strive every day to focus on what is important to me: building strong, healthy relationships with my family and colleagues.

One of the most important features to remember is honesty. You have to be honest with yourself about your goals, interests, and desires. If you do not have a clear understanding of your own needs, then you will never be able to achieve success. It is as simple as that. You have to know where you are headed before you leave the station.

Chapter 2

▲

Though Not Quite Rivaling the Lincoln Memorial in Stature, My Excuses Make a Pretty Impressive Monument to Nothingness

▲

Sparking your passion isn't just a cute marketing slogan or book subtitle, nor is it a lofty philosophical exercise to be reflected *upon* but never acted *on*. Instead, it is about believing that you can determine the type of life you want for yourself as opposed to being a passive participant in that process.

So before we get started, I have to ask: Do you believe that? Do you really believe, deep down inside, that you *can* create the life you want for yourself? Or do you secretly feel—and subconsciously act—as if you are just a passenger on your own journey through life?

It's not a trick question. For far too many of us, the answer is a surprising one. That's because, for as long as we can remember, we've been told that we are in the driver's seat of our own destiny, and yet we find ourselves living to fulfill others' expectations. The parents think you should be married with kids, the friends think you should be settling down by now, and the mother-in-law thinks you should belong to this club or that society and live in this neighborhood. What's worse is when we internalize their expectations. We act like we're strapped into the passenger seat as our lives barrel onward without us.

In this chapter, we transition from the expectations imposed by others to the ones we impose on ourselves every day, and explore what it takes to change our mindset. When we say "I can't" or "I won't," we are making excuses for why possibilities aren't available to us, and are in fact deciding to allow those excuses to smother opportunities that new passions can uncover. My possibilities have to start with "I can." I *can* do whatever it is, and I *will* do it because it's within my abilities. I was interviewed for an award I recently received and they asked me about my career aspirations. I told them that I wanted to be Commissioner of the LPGA, a model, and a fashion designer, in no particular order, when I grow up. The interviewer and people who read it thought it was hilarious, but of course I was totally serious! I may be closer to the commissioner role on my current career path, but I haven't received any offers yet. Plus, I'm only a statuesque 5'9" in my mind, and I've never taken a draping class. Yet, I think all of these careers are doable—I have the wherewithal to be a commissioner, models come in all shapes and sizes, and I can sign up for a draping class to learn how to create my own designs. Getting my mind right and believing in my ability to do something is the first step in the process.

Saying "I can" or "I will" will not always be easy. From the outside looking in to my life, it may *seem* as though it all comes very easily to me. But the truth is that even penning this book is an exercise in mental fortitude, strategy, execution, and endurance. I have an infant, a husband, a full-time job, a growing business, family, and social obligations—the list goes on and on, as I'm sure yours does too. However, I'm committed to writing this book. That's my "I can" and "I will." Practically speaking, the strategy and execution pieces of that mean late nights and super early mornings even when I'm exhausted from work or my daughter's inclination to carry on lengthy baby talk conversations at obscene hours. It means prioritizing, juggling, manufacturing energy, and using lots of concealer to hide the bags under my eyes. It means sacrifice, staying power, and sometimes just plain grit to push through to create and live the life you want.

Making Excuses, Marking Time

Looking back on my life, I realize that those times when I've missed the biggest opportunities, or perhaps not moved along as far as I could have in the time allotted, seem to coincide with a time in my life when I am more focused on making excuses than I am on moving forward.

I like to think of myself as an active, even ambitious person, but I'm also a strategist at heart. Now, as any general can tell you (or any fan of the History and Military History Channels), if you take too long laying out your strategy for how to approach the battlefield, the battle may already be over by the time you send your men in. Likewise, I always like to have a plan and/or strategy. I analyze and mitigate risk for a living, so I am a person who thinks thoroughly through situations. I know that sometimes I get mired in the details. If I'm not purposeful about my analysis, I can miss the forest for the trees and allow the risk I'm evaluating to become the excuse why "I can't." By the time I look up from creating my strategy, I find that the door to that particular opportunity has closed—or has been opened by someone who was doing a little more acting. When I'm purposeful about that same analysis, I recognize the risk and figure out how I can make my goal happen in spite of it.

What many of us do in place of strategy and execution is make excuses:

* "I can't take that college course right now, even though I need it for that promotion at work, because I'm just too busy."

* "I can't exercise today, it's raining!"

* "I know I should be cooking something healthy tonight, but I'm so tired. I'll just go through this drive-through..."

* "I know I should be updating my blog right now, but the season finale is on tonight!"

Most excuses are merely us marking time with our mouths. The solution is often right there in the excuse: I can't do *this* because I have to do *that* instead. And even though most excuses cost us opportunities, we continue to make them anyway.

As you're about to see, these excuses come at a premium price.

Finding Your Discomfort Zone

Life is full of limitations we have no control over—natural disasters, accidents, surprises, shortfalls, detours, obstacles, other people, and the fickle whims of fate all combine to create the setting of our lives, but not the destiny. The antidote to limitation is, of course, choice. Turn left to avoid this obstacle; go right to avoid that one. And yet every day it seems we make choices that limit our own destinies, rather than expand them. And whether we choose *to* do something (watch TV, take a nap, sleep on it) or *not* do something (skip night class, call out of work, ignore our blog or destiny or dream), those choices only serve to put more and more limits on the life we could lead.

Similar to most people, I've been guilty of putting limitations on my own destiny in the past. But throughout the years I have learned to make choices that move me out of that comfort zone of over-strategizing and into the more uncomfortable, yet far less limiting *discomfort* zone. In fact, I've discovered that the more uncomfortable a thought, action, opportunity, or desire makes me, the more I'm going to be drawn to it because, in the past, those opportunities have often paid off the most.

Where Mind Meets Matter: *Your Physical Affects Your Emotional*

One of my strongest beliefs has to do with the body-mind connection. For me, and for so many people today, success is as much about being healthy as it is anything else. It's hard to focus on anything, whether you're passionate about it or not, if you don't feel well or if you don't have the energy. Though logically you recognize the importance of getting your body right, actually doing it is a different matter entirely. Again, much of this involves excuses such as "I don't have time, with work, family, kids, and so on"; "I don't know where to start or what to do to change my body"; "Fitness people are not intelligent or are fanatics"; or "I can't afford it." The fact of the matter is that you are most likely shortchanging yourself on realizing your personal best because you are not taking care of yourself physically and mentally.

I say this as someone who, for a time, was also guilty of shortchanging my physical health. Not only was I overweight for my frame size, but I had also developed a cholesterol issue and faced a family history of diabetes. Even as I recognized these critical health issues, I continued to make excuses about my lifestyle, my work ethic, my attitude, and even my job—particularly when I was working in the professional golfing industry, which involved providing 'round-the-clock hospitality for clients, wining and dining them, and making sure they were fully entertained. I was constantly surrounded by delicious, high-calorie, and fatty cuisine, especially during tournaments and other work-related meetings and events. Instead of taking responsibility for actively working out and controlling what I ate, I simply made excuses for all the weight I was gaining. They weren't even novel excuses! They ran the gamut from "socializing is a part of my job" to "Midwesterners have a different perception of what a healthy weight is." I even went so far as to say, "I would have a fabulous body if only I had my own personal trainer like Madonna and all the time in the world to work out." Eventually, however, I reached that pivotal moment when I realized that my physical shape was affecting my mental abilities, and that I had to stop making excuses and commit to doing something about it.

Without having such an approach in place and by living an imbalanced life, we are sure to lack the necessary focus, vision, and, let's face it, the energy needed to succeed.

One of my strongest passions is the belief that you must take care of yourself physically, mentally, and emotionally. My own will and determination to live a healthier lifestyle originally stemmed from the desire to avoid taking medication or having to experience the health challenges others around me were dealing with. I absolutely did not want to live the rest of my life popping pills to deal with the bad choices I'd made concerning food and fitness, so I devoted myself to making better choices to turn my health—and my life—around. Not only did I reverse the risk of diabetes and high cholesterol I had been facing, but today I now compete in physique and bodybuilding competitions even when confronted with persistent physical challenges. My journey has been an evolution. I needed a mental reboot, of sorts, to overcome my own persistent excuse-making.

The High Cost of Limitations

So, what is the high cost of limitations? The cost is simply not living the life you want to live. I know that the choices I make—to act or *not* act—directly affect my reality. That's why I've moved across the country more than a few times to pursue this opportunity or that. And it may not sound like much, but we all know how disruptive a move—particularly a cross-country move—can be to your comfort zone. I've moved to cites where I didn't know anyone because I felt it was the best opportunity for me at that time. But not everybody feels this way. For instance, I have friends who have been afraid to go outside of the geographical area in which they live. That decision has cost them in terms of pursing their goals because the opportunity just doesn't exist where they currently live. They may be comfortable in their current geographical setting, but I know that stretching into their "discomfort" zone might help to enrich their lives and, quite possibly, help them find their passion as well.

Don't get me wrong: no opportunity is risk-free, and there is much to be said about comfort in life. But is it our destiny to be comfortable? Or to be passionate about the life we live and content that we've made the right choices, even if they were difficult, about our own destinies? In short, don't be so comfortable that your life is free of passion.

Is it always going to be an easy or straight path to success? *No!*

But, is it possible? *Yes!*

The 5 Most Common Types of Excuses We Tell Ourselves to Limit Ourselves

I like to identify the challenges in front of me so that I can work purposefully to avoid them. The same goes for my own limitations. When I feel myself starting to sink into that limiting mindset, I immediately start digging myself out. The only way to do so is to first identify the limitation and then work to eradicate it. I'm not talking about some lofty, super-transcendental, philosophical "I think therefore I am" exercise; I'm talking everyday stuff. For example, at the moment, I'm still working on getting my post-baby body to look like my pre-baby body. (Vain? Maybe. Think my pre-baby-body quest is totally irrelevant to your efforts to find and live your passion? We're talking about excuses in everyday life, so hang with me here.) The pre-baby body requires exercise and eating clean. My challenge? I like snacks, tasty treats, and just about every dessert that exists now or will be created in the future. But I also know that indulging in those heavenly morsels limits my ability to obtain that pre-baby body. I can rationalize indulging by telling myself that I need to reward myself or that a little won't hurt or that I'll start tomorrow. But making those excuses limits or downright sabotages my probability of success.

Let's work on eradicating life's limiting excuses by identifying the **5 Most Common Types of Excuses We Tell Ourselves to Limit Ourselves:**

1. **Time.** Time is one of our biggest excuses. Now more than ever, we are all pressed for time. The technology that was supposed to help us manage our time—e-mail, text messaging, tablets, smart phones, and all the rest—has merely added to our lack of time. But time is also one of the easiest excuses to mitigate. I'm sure if we all looked at our lives, we could find dozens of ways to find more time. Merely watching one less hour of television per day, playing one less game of Candy Crush, or answering one less e-mail or text could add hours to every day. And when there are truly only five minutes left, then you start to prioritize and juggle! It's not a perfect solution but it can help you bridge the gaps.

2. **Money.** Money is often a legitimate excuse, because we only have a finite amount of cash to make things happen. If your passion in life is to direct movies, for example, and you're a 50-year-old middle manager for a fax machine company with a wife, two kids, a mortgage, and childcare payments, it can be a legitimate challenge to pay for four years of film school! And yet, if that's your passion, there is always a way.

3. **Energy.** "I just don't have the energy!" is another often legitimate excuse. In our constantly multitasking modern lives, energy can be one of our first resources to run dry.

4. **Permission.** Not having permission is an excuse we give ourselves when none of the others really apply. For instance, you may have the time, the money, and even the energy, but your resistance to leaving your comfort zone is so strong that you struggle to find an excuse not to, so you look for someone else to validate your passion. The need for third-party validation of your passion as sensible, practical, or functional is often the excuse of last resort.

5. **Bandwidth.** This is one you hear a lot lately, and it's kind of a culmination or catch-all of all the previous excuses. When you say, "I don't have enough bandwidth to take that project on right now," what you're really saying is, "Life is too busy to explore living it the way I prefer." Bandwidth is a legitimate issue; I certainly don't recommend pushing yourself to exhaustion or to the point of a nervous breakdown. However, bandwidth does become an excuse when you use it as the reason to forever abandon exploring your passion.

Excuses exist because sometimes doing what you *want* instead of everything else you *need* to do just isn't practical or responsible. Sometimes we really don't have the money, time, energy, or bandwidth, or we do need to get the buy-in (or the permission) of other stakeholders in our lives to pursue an opportunity to its fullest extent. But when we keep making the same excuses, time and again, year after year, the cost mounts with each missed opportunity. Now we're talking more than mere excuses; we're talking about the sacrifice of living the life you actually want.

So we have to begin asking ourselves some pertinent questions for why these excuses keep recurring:

* Is an extra hour of TV each night more important than starting our own company, taking a class to better ourselves, or working on that business plan?

* Do we need a new car every three years, or can we go for six years and use the car-payment money to open our own business, earn a degree, or otherwise pursue our passion?

* Where are we spending all our energy? Is it in pursuing our passion, or simply running to stand still on a mountain of chores, tasks, and busywork?

* Finally, what—if anything—is more important to us than our passion? And why aren't we making that a priority?

When you connect with the spark that is your passion, trust me, *nothing* will stand in your way. Nothing. Hungry people who chase opportunity even into their discomfort zones will always find their way over, around, under, or sometimes straight through any and every detour, obstacle, challenge, or excuse to see their dream fulfilled.

The Sky Is the Limit—*As Long As It Falls in My Lap!*

Most of us are fine with opportunity, as long as we stumble over it on the way to work or it knocks on our front door! The problem is that it hardly ever—*if* ever—works that way. Instead, we must go and seek out opportunity, even if it eludes us at every turn.

I know life is hard enough without having to hunt down opportunity all the time. But remember what I said earlier about your comfort zone: it might be comfortable, but more often than not our true passion (or at least most opportunities to find it) lies well into our discomfort zone.

Case in point: my husband, Ken, and I are entrepreneurs. We have a business that manufactures and sells **theBulldog Bar**, which is a decorative home security device that goes inside of your house to prevent kick-in home invasions. In the wake of the school shooting tragedies, we've also sold them to secure school safety rooms. We've taken it from an idea to actually making and selling the product domestically; our next goal is to export it. It certainly hasn't been easy, and we still have our challenges, but we're so passionate about it, we didn't want to put off testing the commercial waters any longer.

With any entrepreneur—even if you are Oprah or Bill Gates—there are bottom lines, budgets, and finite resources that you can allocate toward various ideas and opportunities. What we've done in our business is to try to partner with people who are also trying to get their business off of the ground so that when we work together there is a win-win. We try to be as entrepreneurial as we can in terms of how we get things done.

For example, a friend of ours does outside sales work, and he's trying to boost his portfolio, so we work with him on a commission basis. This is a win-win for us because if we get paid, he gets paid. We don't employ him as a full-time salesperson because we don't have the budget to do that...yet. He's been in the business a while and is pricey. But it still works out as a mutually beneficial arrangement that allows us to drive our wholesale and distributor sales without needing the complete infrastructure of a dedicated and salaried sales department.

Rather than saying that "things can't work out" and "we can't do this business because we don't have a full-time wholesale/distributor sales guy," we figured out a temporary bridge to make it work. We have made it work because exploring this idea is a priority for us. The limitations of the conventional way of doing things didn't stop us from pursuing our passion for this particular project, though it would have been easy to make that excuse. It certainly is not easy to get a business off the ground, but if you keep moving and taking steps it will open other doors.

What's important to remember about passion is that it's an internal drive, and those are really, really easy to bury and "excuse" away. As I said, it would have been easy to look at our idea, realize we couldn't fully staff a brick and mortar company, and simply excuse the idea away. But we talked about it, got creative, and refused to make excuses for something that really mattered to us. But remember, this drive doesn't necessarily have to be business-related. I'm really talking about a lifestyle. Let's use something like skiing, for example, which I learned in Minnesota. Now, I did not know how to ski when I moved there, and I had never had any desire to learn, but, as the new kid in town, I'd been around a lot of people who talked about how much fun they had with the sport, and I knew I had to at least try it. Minnesota doesn't have the world's greatest ski slopes, but it is frozen nine months out of the year!

I could have used my inability to ski or the fact that people do break bones while doing it as a great excuse to stay in the house. But instead I used skiing as a way to interact with people. I didn't know anyone other than my coworkers, and I didn't know anything about skiing, so it was a perfect opportunity to meet new friends and explore something that might become a new passion. The ski clubs up there in Minnesota welcomed me with open arms and really helped me get out of my shell, skiing-wise. I'm not going to say skiing was my passion, necessarily, but I've always been interested in trying new things and, above all, proving that I can do something out of my comfort zone, whether that be strapping two sticks to my feet and racing down a hill or making a new city my home without knowing anyone there.

You can't let what you've always done be an excuse for why you can't do something else. Passion-sparking is about trying new things because you never know what you'll like. It's about taking positive steps forward, moving past the excuses to figure out the action plan that will get you over challenges and humps to where you need be in life.

The ROI of Risk-Taking

What is it about risk-taking that makes folks so uncomfortable? Well, risk equals new, unexpected, uncertain, unsure...what *isn't* there to feel uncomfortable about?

More than anything else, I think risk means that you may lose something that you have. It can be a house, a job, a savings account, a career, or even a reputation or credibility. When those kinds of things are on the table, it makes people very uncomfortable indeed. And rightfully so. In no way, shape, or form am I suggesting that you quit your day job tomorrow and go climb Mount Everest, open a dance studio, direct a movie, or go back to college...unless that is your absolute passion in life and you have an executable strategy by which you can make it happen.

What I am talking about is calculated risk-taking. I'm not the type of person who goes to Vegas to gamble because in my mind that is a bad calculated risk. Why? Because my goal is to win, and in Vegas, the house always wins. I'm not going to engage in that kind of random, uncalculated risk that means I will most surely lose eventually.

I do find value in risk-taking because I believe if you always do what you've always done, then you'll always get what you've always got(ten). Sure, life may be safer that way—and certainly more comfortable—but I believe you're reading this book because you're ready for more than comfort. I believe you have to wrap your mind around taking some risks and taking chances if there is a reason to believe that the payoff is going to propel you forward.

The "calculated" part in risk-taking comes when you inform yourself and do your homework to the point where you know, understand, and have evaluated the risk, but determined that there is a big enough ROI—Return On Investment—and go for it anyway.

As an example, let's go back to being an entrepreneur: My husband and I are both busy professionals and parents, and we have our fair share of excuses when it comes to time, money, energy, permission, and bandwidth. But we are also really, really passionate about the work we're doing with our security business. Now, since we made some basic, simple decisions—for instance, working with an on-commission salesperson instead of hiring one full-time, and running the business end from our home for now—we were able to take a calculated risk versus a bigger risk. We could have run off half-cocked and rented out a fancy office suite in some commercial park, decked it all out with big desks and chairs and a sitting room and all-leather furniture and framed wall art, but instead we hedged our bets carefully and are proceeding slowly.

Meet *Marc Lamont Hill*

Ten years ago, Marc Lamont Hill was living on the streets of Atlanta when another homeless person told him he did not belong there. Marc revealed to this homeless person that he wanted to get his PhD, but that the process takes way too long. In response, the homeless person told him that 10 years were going to pass no matter what, so the only question Marc needed to ask himself was whether or not he was going to have the PhD he desired so much at the end of it.

What's so great about Marc's story is the power of the excuses he was telling himself. And, truth be told, many were legitimate. Homeless and without transportation, going to school for 10 years must have seemed like an insurmountable task at the time. But as his homeless friend pointed out, "You've got nothing to lose; those 10 years are going to go by anyway." So all of Marc's excuses just kind of fell away, one by one, in his mind: If he didn't have transportation, there was the bus. If he didn't have money, there was financial aid. If he didn't have clean clothes, there were programs to help with that. If he didn't have a place to shower, there was the YMCA. Every time he made another excuse, his friend's words came back to him, until finally Marc's passion was sparked and he was ready to take that calculated risk and follow his dreams.

The rest, as they say, is history. Today Dr. Marc Hill is on the faculty at Columbia University, is the author of not one but two books, is the editor-at-large for the Philadelphia *Daily News*, and is a regular commentator for CNN, MSNBC, and the Fox News Channel.

Marc's inspiring story proves that it is only our excuses that prevent us from realizing everything we were meant to be. At the end of the day, no matter what your situation is, you've got to figure out what matters to you, and work for it.

Parting Words

I have made my fair share of excuses and put dozens of limits upon myself throughout the years. And yet, in general, I have the mindset that I can achieve anything if I put my mind to it. So, from an academic and professional standpoint, I have never struggled with "I can't" as much as "You can't." In other words, my struggle has always been, "How do I work my way around *you telling me that I can't?*"

The worlds I work in—corporate board rooms, professional sports, and home security—are male-dominated, and I've certainly run into more than my fair share of obstacles and challenges that don't necessarily apply to my male counterparts. But these worlds are where my passion is, and I'm not going to let my own excuses or those of others hold me back. We all have legitimate excuses that stand in our way, but finding your passion and living your truest life is about moving forward anyway, and overcoming those obstacles.

You are worth it, and life is what you make of it. Remember that excuses are like potholes in your journey toward success: there is always a way around them if you just slow down and look hard enough!

Chapter 3

Risk-Taking Is the Secret Ingredient of a Purposeful Life

I talk a lot about risk because I believe that it truly is the secret ingredient of a purposeful life—even though the concept of taking risks isn't exactly a secret. We all know how we feel about risk. It's uncomfortable and downright scary because it means we can fail and lose everything we've already accomplished. But mustering the courage to step out of our comfort zones and branch out into new and uncharted territory is what separates those who are just surviving from those who are thriving in a life of power, purpose, and passion.

The Power of Taking Risks

I'm a strong believer in calculated risk-taking because I have personally benefited more from taking risks than from not taking them. And when I say "benefit," I'm talking about much more than just a return on my investment; I've been rewarded with a more powerful, passionate, and purposeful life.

Looking back on my life so far, I smile with satisfaction to see the risks I've taken that resulted in some of my most incredible and rewarding experiences. Case in point: I worked as a lawyer for the Ladies Professional Golf Association (LPGA) for nearly six years. Is that an industry I would have ever guessed I would be a part of? Not at all. In fact, I wasn't a golf aficionado when this opportunity presented itself, but there was a draw, an appeal there for me that proved powerful to resist. Not only would I be the first African-American lawyer on any golf tour ever, but I felt I was helping to break down barriers and increasing exposure for other folks as well.

Professionally speaking, it was a big time commitment during the growth years of my career, and risky in the sense that I was breaking new ground, personally and professionally. Six years in the wrong industry would have had pretty high costs for my growth as an attorney, but six years in the right one would rapidly accelerate my passion, potential, and purpose. So although it was a risky career move in an unproven profession, it had a high ROI that I'm still reaping to this day.

That said, I also made the move for my own personal development. It was a new industry to me, a new sport, and new people to meet. Along the way I gained great experience, such as winning a five-country intellectual property dispute that spanned the course of five years; an experience I would not have dreamed of if I had never taken that initial risk and said, "Let's try it and see what there is to learn." It really gave me some opportunities to grow and develop that I wouldn't have known otherwise if I had stayed in my comfort zone and not taken the calculated risk to grow, personally and professionally.

I know taking risks can be hard. I know that we're all older and wiser now and have more to lose than some skin off our knee if we fall off our bike. But our lives aren't over and every day above ground requires just a little risk, don't you think? And sometimes, chasing after our passions requires more than a little.

Calculating Risk: *The Secret Ingredient's Secret Ingredient!*

I hesitate to call this a "self-help" book because I've seen that term used so often in relation to books that really don't help anyone but the author promote his or her cause and/or career. And I say that with due respect to any author because I know writing a book is not easy. It's a great responsibility, not just in putting words on a page, but in trying to guide someone—in this case you, the reader—to a higher truth she may not have realized before opening your book. I don't believe a lot of self-help books are, in fact, very helpful because they *are* simply words on a page, exhorting you to:

* Buy a house, fix it up, and "flip" your way into an early retirement.

* Become a day trader and retire at 29.

* Picture yourself holding the steering wheel of a Lamborghini and the car will magically appear in your driveway.

I believe that, as adults, we all know better than that. Or at least we should. However, when we're vulnerable, when we're desperate, when we're down and just need that one big break to make everything "right," we're not thinking with our brains but with our hearts. It's those situations and on those bases when risk-taking becomes dangerous and, in some cases, disastrous.

How many well-meaning, hardworking, good-hearted and good-intentioned people bought up as much real estate as they could just before the bubble burst, and watched it all disappear in the blink of an eye? And how many of them got the idea from a $10 self-help book that all their friends were reading or that the host of their favorite TV show bragged about? How many people quit good jobs to trade in the stock market only to watch their dreams disappear with the first big market fluctuation, let alone the next big crash? How many people are still waiting for that sports car in their driveway after they've pictured it and visualized it almost to death?

And how many opportunities to actually go out, pursue their passion, and earn a sports car for themselves have they passed up along the way while keeping their eyes shut and their dreams big? Don't get me wrong, dreaming—and even visualization—are powerful tools for a richer, more passionate life. But in almost every case, dreams are the starting line for a purposeful life, not the finish line, for dreams alone can't propel you to success or purpose. Instead, what happens in *between* your dreams and your reality are the steps you take to make it so, and those are always action steps.

The idea of passion-sparking is critical in finding your life's ultimate purpose, and our purpose often involves risk of some sort. Maybe it's not jumping out of an airplane or racing around a track at 300 miles per hour, but when you've got a spouse, 2.5 kids, and a 30-year, fixed-rate mortgage hanging over your heads, even a little risk can feel like leaping out of a Lear jet without a parachute! That's because as we get older, life cements us to a certain job, career, address, and routine, and it gets harder and harder—and riskier and riskier—to act upon our passion. How many people do we know (including ourselves) who, in high school or college, tried hard to pursue their true passion, calling, or purpose—it might have been acting, writing, singing, zoology, archaeology, or philosophy—only to have a rude awakening upon graduation: the world needs more garbage men than philosophers.

After going on dozens of auditions or interviews or casting calls or callbacks or job fairs, we feel the mounting pressure of our credit card and student loan debts and so we do what most people do: we take the first job offered to us. And we tell ourselves we'll work hard, save up, go back to school, keep auditioning, keep sending out demo tapes or taking philosophy courses to get our doctorate, and then...we meet someone. We fall in love, we marry, we move in together, we buy a house, we have a child or two, and with every life change comes more and more responsibility. Most of it is happy stuff, good stuff: parenting and being in love and building a home and putting down roots and watching your child or spouse blossom and grow are all positive, life-affirming events, but they also take time, energy, and valuable resources away from our own passion.

Don't Learn to Take Risks, Re-Learn

Think back to childhood and you will soon realize that risk-taking is part of our human DNA. Everything we do as children involves a risk of some sort. We don't know if we'll be able to stand on these things we call legs, but we're tired of sitting so we decide to get up one day, and, after a few tumbles, we do it! We don't know if we'll ever be able to walk, but we're tired of crawling so we grab a coffee table or a chair leg, haul ourselves up, and set off on a grand adventure, even if it only lasts for a few steps before we take another tumble.

Every day is like that, full of firsts and tries and failures and successes, from standing to crawling to walking to running to riding a bike to the first day of kindergarten to tasting your first vegetable or cookie.

And with each new development, each passing year, we grow a little wiser. Some risks pay off, others not so much. Touching that red-hot burner wasn't such a good idea, was it? Biting into that lemon because you thought it would taste like an orange didn't work out either. Then the risks get a little bigger, with higher costs if they don't pan out. Asking your first date to a dance only to hear a no? Ouch, that rejection really hurt. Running for class president only to lose? Zing, another painful wound that will take time to heal.

We are born risk-takers, but life gradually "un-teaches" us this skill. With each failed risk, we shrink back from the experience—and the opportunity another risk might provide. I think we all know people who took a few risks in their youth and, frankly, never got over them. Maybe they still have relationship issues, confidence issues, or other issues they're still working out that affect their very future despite the initial event being decades gone. How many times can we fail before we stop taking risks altogether? The fact is, we all try, and we all fail. In fact, statistically speaking, the more you try the more you will fail, which can be depressing if you forget that each failure is a lesson.

The older we get, the more attached we are to the lives of others—family, friends, spouses, children, mortgages, college funds, braces, and so on— the more failure becomes more than a lesson, and the more we actually have to lose. It's a lot easier to take risks in high school or college where the only thing we really have to lose is a little face, or confidence.

But our lives don't end when we are "married with children." The point I want to make in this section is that life goes on, with or without risk. But I believe you purchased a book called *Life at the Speed of Passion* because you are ready, willing, and able to add a little more risk to your life. And I want you to, but I want you to do it in a calculated way so that your chances of success increase with each risk you take, and don't decrease instead.

So this is not an issue of learning how to take risks. Anyone who can ride a bike without skinning their knee or tie their shoe has tried something new or taken a risk. What I'm urging you to do is re-learn how to take risks, not living in fear of what might happen but using the wisdom you've gained from every life experience to reduce the cost of each risk you take from this day forward.

That's right; we're grown! So just think how much more we know now than we did as kids, watching our dads taking off our training wheels and wondering how we're ever going to ride a bike without them.

We need to recognize and, just as importantly, trust the knowledge we have and be bigger than the fear of risk to follow our passion with confidence and courage.

The Two Components of Calculated Risk-Taking

There are two vital components that go together to form a calculated risk:

1. Attitude
2. Outlook readjustments

Attitude

When it comes to your attitude, you have to understand that life is not like the movies, but each of us is writing our own screenplay. Hollywood endings aren't realistic, but neither is hiding in the shadows because you're too scared to risk living a bigger, brighter, happier, more purposeful life. We may not all become astronauts or movie stars or opera divas or supermodels, but we all have hopes, dreams, passions, and promise yet to be achieved. But we can't achieve anything if we don't believe in ourselves.

Pessimism is not an option when it comes to passion and purpose. You must believe that you can achieve if you hope to act on your passion with a balanced, realistic, and grown-up plan. You have to balance incredible optimism with credible realism. Part of my job, every day, is mitigating risk as life's various opportunities come my way. But you can't do that if your every thought is, "This will never work." You can't see the world with rose-colored glasses, ignoring the risk of every opportunity, but you can't hide your head in the sand and avoid every opportunity either. As I said earlier, you've got to get comfortable with being uncomfortable.

There will be times when things look bleak. I know because I have those times too. Author bios are great because you can list all your accomplishments, but I don't believe I've ever seen a list of their failures. Who wants to read about that? But I've had my share; we all have. The difference between walking away a failure and turning that failure into a success is learning to combat your pessimism with habitual optimism. You have to say, think, and believe, "I can do this. There's no good reason why I can't." Make optimism a daily habit.

I use a variety of tricks to keep my spirits up and ready to face risk at a moment's notice. For instance, there is just something about music that moves me and really lifts my spirit. So if I'm bummed out or feeling negative, I have certain playlists that consistently work to lift my mood and put my head back in the game. I also use positive self-talk. Yes, you read that right—I talk to myself. Aloud or just in my head, I'll repeat over and over, until I believe it, "I absolutely can," and, "Of course I will." I believe if you say those things out loud it really does affect your outlook on the situation. Just beware of the other side of that coin: negative self-talk affects your outlook too.

Outlook Adjustments

In addition to adjusting your attitude, from time to time you will need to adjust your outlook. Your attitude about daily opportunities and risk slowly seeps into your outlook on life in general. That's why confidence and optimism need to be habitual: what you do every day becomes what your days, weeks, months and years are about. If your everyday attitude is, "I'm not worth it, I'm not smart enough, I could never do that, I'm not good enough," then your mind will start to believe it and your actions will reflect it. Never underestimate the power of negative self-talk and how strong that vibe can get if you continually put yourself down and limit your life based on unfair and unproven beliefs about your limitless potential.

I don't know you and I'm not going to toss out generic platitudes based on some cookie-cutter template, but if you're reading these words then I know you want more, which means you're capable of more. "More" is rarely easy and that path to purpose is not always a straight one. Could I tell you that I always wanted exactly what I've achieved in my life? No, because the road I took to get here was filled with switchbacks, detours, potholes, and sharp turns. What I *could* tell you is that I started out with a specific goal and have always kept my eyes on that particular prize. That is, I always wanted to be a lawyer, and that powerful purpose of mind led to different opportunities along my own individual journey. Each time, as I gained exposure and learned from my own and other people's experiences, I readjusted my outlook to approach the next phase of my journey.

Your journey is not over, despite what your negative self-talk may have told you. You are on your journey, not at the end of it, and my hope for you is that this is a critical crossroads where you can step back, see the paths in front of you, and take the positive, perhaps even riskier one, toward a different, more powerful, passionate, and purposeful journey.

Learn from your past, embrace your present, and plan for your future by adjusting your outlook to be more positive, open, and receptive, not just to risk but to change itself. Every so often along your journey you have to adjust your outlook and be flexible enough to modify your course to do those things you must to achieve success.

Speaking of success, let me introduce you to Scott Duffy, risk-taker extraordinaire.

Meet *Scott Duffy*

Scott Duffy is a high-energy executive and serial entrepreneur. Duffy started his career working with best-selling author and speaker Anthony Robbins. He was an executive and Early Stage Manager at FoxSports.com, NBC Internet, CBS Sports line, and Quote.com, where he led teams through their startup phase, fundraising, mergers and acquisitions, and initial public offerings. Recently, he created and launched Smart Charter, an online booking tool that makes it easy to buy and sell trips on a private jet. His company is often referred to as "Expedia for private aviation." Scott sold the company to Richard Branson's Virgin Group. The company was re-branded as Virgin Charter and named "One of Fifteen Companies That Will Change the World" by CNN Money.

What's amazing about Scott isn't so much his destination, which is impressive, but his journey. As a serial entrepreneur, Scott's job description is one word: risk.

There are no guarantees with start-up companies, and Scott has started, grown, and sold his fair share, even before Smart Charter/ Virgin Charter. Having spoken with Scott for this book, I can tell you he's no daredevil, but simply a man charged with passion for various projects, and unwilling to let discomfort stand in the way of opportunity.

Parting Words: *The Rewards of Discomfort*

Let me sum up this section by saying this: *risk is a part of life.* You can't avoid it, you can't run from it, you can't hide from it, you can only delay it. Every time we get behind the wheel, take a flight, or simply step into an elevator, we are risking our very lives. And yet we do such things without a second thought because, statistically speaking, they are considered "safe." Although we all have something to protect, I'm not convinced that a life filled with power, passion, and purpose is supposed to be safe. I'm not saying we should put our family's security at risk every day, but sometimes to reap a bigger gain we must calculate the risk and take a chance on the unexpected, the uncertain, even the unknown.

No change comes without cost, even if the "price" is simply a little comfort along the way. Hopefully by now we've learned a little more about the costs of comfort and the rewards of discomfort—and how to balance the two for a more passionate, purposeful life!

Chapter 4

Thank Goodness Someone Else Invented the Wheel So I Can Bypass That Whole Chisel-and-Stone Business

The one thing I'd like you to take away from this book is that passion is not a destination, but a journey. Life is not static; it is continually changing, evolving, and growing along with the rest of us. Just as our bodies change from, say, our 20s and 30s to our 40s and 50s, so too do our passions. What inspired you in your teens—maybe a passion for drawing or creating elaborate fantasy worlds—may evolve in your 20s and 30s to being a children's book illustrator or painting wall murals for your local community.

Although it would be nice to do one thing and do it well for the rest of your life, the fact is that most of us don't work that way. We are continually jumping tracks from inspiration to inspiration, flitting here and there. So I don't think we necessarily have to be limited to one passion. We can have different ones throughout our life, and we don't necessarily have to be struck by only one epiphany about what we want to be in our life.

For example, my journey has been diverse and surprising, mainly because I allow myself to be open to passion as well as to pushing the pause button—or even the delete button—if something isn't working out for me or I don't feel it's destined to be my purpose. So I give myself permission to get jazzed about something and then try it and see if I like it. If not, I'll move on. I may get passionate about such personal interests as hat making and draping and learn as much about them as I can or maybe take a class or two, but I won't necessarily throw myself into them or sign up for a degree program.

We all have the capacity for much more than staying in one little box all our lives. That's what I mean by passion-sparking: figuring out all of those things you can do through trial and error until your fire is stoked and you're being purposeful and passionate about whatever it is you do, for as long as you wish to do it.

Why Reinvent the Wheel?

When I want to figure out and experience new things for myself from a professional standpoint, rather than reinventing the wheel and painstakingly learning from every one of my own trials and errors, I can hitch my wagon to someone else's horse for a bit to learn what he or she has done that I can use to expedite my growth in my pursuit of the same goals. I can gain inspiration and information from what others—such as savvy entrepreneur Scott Duffy—have done to inform and inspire my own journey, and more quickly reach my goals. I will ultimately have to take those steps myself and achieve success on my own terms, in my own way, and on my own timeline, but I won't have to stop my life and switch tracks to do so because I can apply the lessons learned and mistakes made by others to my own unique situation.

In fact, I believe that the more mentors and non-mentors I seek out and query about their projects, passions, purpose, and potential, the more experiences I can gain that inform my own journey. When I tell people I'm interested in what they are doing and what they think they did right and what they maybe didn't, I find that people are pretty open about sharing what worked and what didn't work for them.

I certainly have to consider the source and factor in who that individual is, but, ultimately, I am able to apply that learning and experience to my life without actually experiencing it for myself. It's no different from asking a good friend or colleague who recently visited Hawaii about the best places to stay, eat, and explore when you're planning your own trip. Why trust a guidebook or make expensive mistakes by just showing up and blindly guessing?

The same principle can be applied to any field, passion, purpose, or endeavor. If you're going to start a restaurant of your own, wouldn't you want to talk to a handful of restaurateurs who've had ups, downs, and in-betweens to know what to expect before investing your life's savings and making the same mistakes, but at a much higher cost?

I find that this puts me much farther ahead of the game because I've already walked a mile in someone else's shoes to avoid stubbing my own toe! So as we start to figure out what our own personal and professional lifestyle might look like, we can use that overlay of experience in our strategy to pursue our passions.

How to Shorten Your Learning Curve in 3 Simple Steps

If you don't happen to be one of those people who was struck by an epiphany of your life's passion and how to achieve it at the age of 10, figuring out what exactly you are passionate about and how to make it happen may take some legwork on your part. But you can shorten your path to purpose by shortening your learning curve. I've outlined the three simple steps you can take to make that happen:

1. Narrow your focus.

2. Ask questions.

3. Set a goal.

Step 1: *Narrow Your Focus*

The first step in shortening your learning curve is to narrow your focus. For instance, if someone were to come up to me and say, "Tell me how to become a success," I wouldn't have an answer right away because that isn't a good question to elicit the information that will be most helpful to her. The formal and informal skill-sets that would make you a successful sports lawyer, for example, are different from those that might make you a successful pole dancer, chef, or lobbyist.

But if someone were to approach me and say, "Eve, I know you have a lot of experience in sports; how could I make it in this business as a woman?" Or, "What's it like being an entrepreneur?" Then, I would have an unlimited amount of experience to share with them, and my answers would be much more targeted.

So the first step is to find out what interests you at the moment, and then go on from there. This may involve a little soul-searching on your own. For instance, you might say music interests you. Okay, great start. But what specifically about the music industry are you most passionate about? Is it:

* Performing?
* Setting up the stage?
* Writing music?
* Marketing music?
* Designing album covers?
* Directing music videos?

Your answers to these questions will help you get ready to ask the next set of questions.

Step 2: *Ask Questions*

I always say a question is worth a thousand experiences because asking the right question—and we're going to learn how to do that in this chapter—can truly save you lots of time, energy, resources, and money. Asking the right question can help you get exposure to things that you ordinarily wouldn't be exposed to, and provide answers to questions you might never have thought to ask.

Once you've accomplished Step 1 and have figured out what interests you, you can begin to form intelligent questions that will help shorten your learning curve.

Just as an example, let's say that in your Step 1 exercise, you realized that you love the marketing and promotions side of entertainment the most. Great, so now you can start leveraging other peoples' experiences by asking those who know something about this field all they have to tell you. You can ask questions such as,

* How did you break into the industry?

* What would you do differently if you could do it all over again?

* What would you do the same?

* If you knew then what you know now, what would your advice be?

* What type of skillset, certification, or degree do you need?

* How would you position yourself?

* How do you recommend I position myself?

Be sure to consider the source and put his or her answers in perspective. For instance, whereas everyone in a certain industry can provide valuable information, not everyone can provide it at the same level. If you're talking to an intern at a radio station, be sure to weigh what he has to say against the advice of someone with a lot more experience, such as a station manager.

The thing about questions is that you don't know what you don't know until you start asking questions—personally or professionally. Through asking good, targeted questions you are going to figure out whether or not X, Y, or Z career is something you would like to do.

Step 3: *Set a Goal*

Finally, once you've narrowed your field of interest and asked a million and one questions to shorten your learning curve, set a goal. It can be low-level or high-level: something fairly simple that you can accomplish in a day, such as filling out the paperwork required to intern at a radio station or marketing firm, or something high-level such as getting a specialized degree in entertainment marketing or completing a six-month internship at a local TV station.

Goal-setting—and reaching—is an important part of the passion-sparking process because it gives your dreams feet. At this stage you start to put action behind your words, thoughts, and intentions and move purposefully and practically toward something you definitely want to achieve.

Overcoming Your Fear of Failure

If there is one universal truth in life, it is this: *Nobody wants to fail.* The desire not to be a failure in the eyes of society, family, and friends is an especially great motivator for me. I mean, if I knew nobody would see me fall on my butt, I would probably try a few more things each year. That's because, from a personal standpoint, I am a person who does not want to fail—ever. There are certainly things I've tried and failed at, and while they've left me determined to succeed anyway, they've definitely reminded me just how much I hate to fail!

Even when I was competing in something personal that didn't make a difference in my professional success, I still "failed" in the sense that I didn't win the event. But rather than never trying anything new for fear of failing, I believe in putting things in perspective: I think failure is actually part of the goal-setting process. I might sulk for a minute after hitting a challenge, roadblock, obstacle, or even outright failure, but there is always a silver lining. That's why teamwork and emotional support are so important. If you surround yourself with other people who support you, they can help you put failures and challenges into perspective, and that can help you set up your success for next time. Doing something wrong one time can also help you modify and adjust your strategy for your next try.

Failure is a two-sided coin. For some people it can be a great motivator to do things right the next time; for others, it can paralyze them because they begin to actively fear failure. Let's say you take a financial risk, for example, and lose your initial investment. Ouch, that's not the kind of failure you'll go rushing back to try again anytime soon. But maybe that failure was because you didn't calculate the risk and instead just rushed into something without having all the information. Are you going to do that again? Not likely. If you are going to try investing again, you'll likely get much more informed first. Some people may not process it that way; they'll just give up on that particular passion because the fear of failure—losing another investment of time, energy, or money—is just too great for them to contemplate ever trying again.

We have to learn to view failure in perspective. Every successful person fails at something; I don't care who they are. Every successful person you'll read about in this book, including myself, has failed on more than one occasion. But we keep going because we've learned to assess failure for what it is, learn from it, and not re-create those same conditions again. And sometimes, what you consider a failure really isn't. Sometimes, what you consider a failure can actually be a success in the eyes of another. Say you commit to finishing a full marathon, but only make it for 18 miles. Well, technically you failed, but what if your neighbor—who watched you train all those months—got so inspired she goes out and runs a marathon herself? That's a success in anybody's book—yours and hers! This is exactly what happened to me with my fitness competitions. I entered to challenge myself and take my fitness to another level. I've competed in a few but didn't win. Even though I didn't come home with a fancy trophy to commemorate my accomplishments, I can't tell you how many of my friends, family, and colleagues were so motivated by my efforts that they committed to improving their health.

The fact is, we don't live our lives in isolation, and many of our successes, if not entirely group efforts, do have ripple effects that influence the lives of those in our immediate and not-so-immediate circles. So what may feel like failure to us looks like success to a lot of other people.

Purpose Isn't a Destination, But a Journey

I'm still discovering my purpose. I enjoy what I do for a living, but it is not just about the work and seeing it as a finish line. What really makes me happy about my job are the dynamics of the workplace, the interplay of the people I work with, and the complexity of what I do every day—and the environment I do it in. I have come to realize that it is those dynamics of what I do every day that work for me, rather than the industry alone.

So basketball and golf and other sports are cool, but the environment of who I work with, the projects I work on, and the autonomy I'm given to be a self-starter are the things that really excite me and determine my path. That may explain why I am also an entrepreneur, because those are the things I tend to be most passionate about from a lifestyle perspective.

Even with the success I have been fortunate enough to experience in my life, I am still exploring new things, even if they are merely personal passions such as draping or hat making, skiing, or traveling. Sometimes they are lofty goals and sometimes they aren't, and that's okay. It took me a while to realize that I wasn't just one thing, and one thing wasn't me; that I could explore and conquer and even fail at a variety of jobs, skills, passions, and pursuits, and that was okay for me.

A lot of times life—and our passion—doesn't live up to our expectations. Say you wanted so badly to become a teacher in your college years, but after your first few years of teaching you realize that standing in front of a room of 35 kids isn't as satisfying as talking to one kid at a time. So you learn, reassess, and adapt. Maybe you go back to school and become a counselor, or you hang your shingle as a private tutor or open a charm school. Whatever you do, know that that is not the *only* thing you can do or will ever do.

Passion is a journey, not a destination, and we are all on it until we're no longer around. I am still working on it and working on it and working on it some more. This book is part of my journey, not my final destination. Once I stopped thinking about what other people wanted me to do or how they wanted me to perform, that is when I finally allowed myself to start finding out what my passion was...and pursuing it with purpose!

Meet *Max Siegel*

I have known Max Siegel since I was in college. He was one of my first mentors and still is to this day. Maybe the reason we connected so early, and so strongly, was because we have both been able to break through and excel in industries not traditionally accessible to African Americans. For instance, he started out as a sports and entertainment lawyer whose clients included prominent artists, athletes, and record labels.

He became the president of Jive for Zomba records (a Sony BMG Company), which was the Gospel label, and turned that business around in less than six years from losing money to making record-breaking profits. Siegel was the only African American who served as a label president under the Sony BMG umbrella at that time.

He was subsequently appointed president of the Dale Earnhardt companies, launched his own race team and sports marketing company, and he is currently the CEO of USA Track and Field.

Parting Words

When it comes to my passion, or even my profession, I confess that I didn't foresee myself sitting in this place. But as I grew and learned and evolved and took on more responsibilities and spoke to more people about various opportunities and strategies, I was ultimately able to reach the place where I am now.

Certainly I've had mentors who played a signifi-cant role in my personal and professional development (you've just met one in Max Siegel), but I have also taken a bit from most of the people I have come in contact with, so in a way nearly everyone I've ever done business with, engaged with, or learned something from has been a mentor of some sort. From finding the best sewing machine for my current hobby to asking a noted CEO how to negotiate effectively, I've learned things from my mentors that, in turn, helped me mentor others by of-fering my own advice, tips, and strategies so that they wouldn't have to reinvent the wheel either.

Through each question asked and answered, I have been able to shorten my learning curve in a variety of industries and at various levels of expertise. It wasn't al-ways easy. Learning the right questions to ask is critical in getting the best answers and the information that will be the most meaningful for you. For instance, a big part of my job is negotiating, and early on in my career I needed help with this, so I asked questions of anyone and every-one I respected in the field of negotiation. I have been very fortunate to encounter folks who are good at that particular skill and who have shared with me how to re-act in different situations, walking me through different aspects of the skill set until I was proficient in it myself. I took what they told me and put my own unique spin on it, learning my own strengths and weaknesses along the way.

In every skill set I conquer, I follow the three steps I've shared with you in this chapter to master it and then move on. It is a simple yet effective way of learning a new skill in a much shorter time span than merely learning through trial and error. There is still some trial and error to experience in every new skill, but finding an area of interest, asking questions, and forming a goal helps shorten the learning curve to succeed sooner.

Some people say there are no shortcuts in life, but I disagree. Although there is no substitute for personal experience, it can be accentuated and even complemented by finding talented people and picking their brains through targeted Q & A sessions. It can shorten the learning curve and allow you to achieve your desired goals faster and, dare I say, better than simple trial and error, which leaves out the impact of other peoples' experiences altogether.

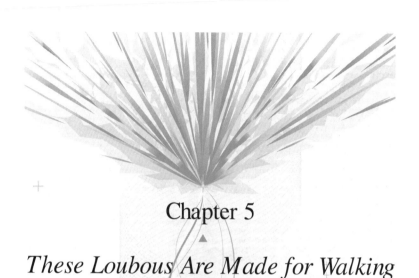

Chapter 5

These Loubous Are Made for Walking

The harder you try, the more opportunities will come to you. The drawback of that truism is that increasing the number of opportunities means that you may fail more often. The only real secret to never failing is to never try, but that's not about passion, that's about defeat.

Even once you've had success at the highest level, there will still be jobs you apply for and don't get. Case in point: I recently applied to be a part of the Executive Leadership Council, or ELC. It's a very prestigious group, and, in my quest for personal and professional excellence, is an organization I believed I could add value to, and derive value from, as a member. Apparently the ELC didn't agree, and I was given a courteous "good luck with life" letter. I have achieved significant feats in my life, I believe, and have received many glowing accolades, and yet this organization that I coveted turned me down. It stung a bit, but I haven't given up.

Setbacks *do* happen, and this was one of mine—hardly the first, nor, if I'm being realistic, the last. My career, though impressive to some, has been riddled with setbacks, challenges, road blocks, and objective failures. Those setbacks and even failures hurt, and yet the sun still rose the next day. Rejection and disappointment always sting for a minute, but then you have to put your life in perspective and move on. That's why the "outlook adjustment" I wrote about earlier in this book is so critical: once you shift your negative outlook you can see that this is just a temporary glitch you can move beyond. So you put one foot in front of the other and keep moving toward achieving your goal.

That's what I have done. It would have been great to have been acknowledged as a member of the ELC or to have received offers for the other positions that turned me down, but I had to realize that each position wasn't ultimately for me because I would not have been positioned for where I am now. That is the point of this chapter: *remaining aware of and attuned to the fact that everything—even the things we view as setbacks— are actually opportunities.*

I believe every setback is a fork in the road where we are faced with two different directions. One direction leads back to our comfort zone, where it's easy to retreat after a disappointment, failure, or setback. Many people take that route, because it's easier. But the other direction is toward uncertainly, anxiety, and another opportunity. It's harder, because it might not be as paved or well-lit as the road back to comfort, disappointment, and another pity party. But to succeed, you must take that more uncertain, more opportune direction.

Even if it looks like a rocky, uphill climb, you have to find the next stepping stone to the next opportunity. In the end, it's not about how fast you get there or even where you end up. Ultimately, sparking your passion and leading a fulfilling life—on your own terms—is all about perception and having a positive outlook.

A Positive Perception Changes Everything

I'm never one to brag, because I believe the minute you poke out your chest in pride is when life comes along to poke you back once or twice to show you what life's really about. But, yes, along my career path and professional journey I've received some pretty fantastic, and even rare accolades that have filled me with pride. But I have to keep it in perspective so that it doesn't change who I am and what I'm trying to achieve with my life. The surest way to bump your head against the ceiling of your own dreams is for your head to get so big it won't fit through the door opportunity is knocking on!

I've learned the hard way that success isn't about what others think of you, but what you think of yourself. For me, those accolades and accomplishments meant I'm on the right path, because every achievement is another tool in my box. The higher I go, the more tools I'm going to need to deal with the inevitable challenges that come with success.

Ultimately, the path you've walked is about acquiring the things you need for your ultimate goal, whatever that may be.

Learning Opportunities Are Still Opportunities

Think of an actress who struggles with audition after audition, for all kinds of parts: the temptress, the bad girl, the studious girl, the athlete, the vampire—whatever it may be. And each time she studies and prepares, learns her lines, goes in, gives it her best shot...and fails. Time after time, year after year, she fails. And then, one day, she gets a call to audition for a role she never thought she'd want: the role of someone who's bitter from life's disappointments and feels like a loser. It's a great role, from a great best-selling book, for a great director...the role of a lifetime. And you know what? She doesn't have to prepare for this audition, because she's already lived the role!

Every failure, every setback, every heartbreak, every "big break" that got broken before this has prepared her—has given her the tools—she needs to succeed. And she nails it, big-time, and success is finally hers. Not because she got "lucky" or because opportunity knocked once, but because she kept going and took every failure as a learning opportunity. Because remember, even learning opportunities are still opportunities. But you'll never find them if you don't go out in search of them. If I'd waited for opportunity to knock at my door, I'd have no door for it to knock on because I would have had no career to pay for a house to hang a door on!

And yet that's exactly what a lot of people do: bide their time, in some cases their whole lives, waiting for opportunity to come to them. There are far too many people in this world who are unwilling to go in search of opportunities. They expect everything to come to them, and, when that doesn't happen, they become disenchanted with their lives. Disenchantment grows to become bitterness. They label others who have succeeded as being "lucky" to have met the right people at the most opportune time, when, in reality, that luck was generated by the conscientious effort of embracing all opportunities and new relationships as they presented themselves.

I always shake my head when the media calls someone—such as an athlete, an author, a singer, a dancer, an actor, or a director—an "overnight success," because if you look closely, if you read their biography or dig a little deeper, you'll find that they've often been working very, very hard for a number of years, maybe even decades, at their chosen profession before they got "lucky" and became that "overnight" success!

What is luck? As the great inventor Thomas Edison once said, "Opportunity is missed by most people because it is dressed in overalls and looks like work." What's more, opportunities can only be cashed in if the person they're presenting themselves to is ready, willing, and able to take that giant leap of faith required.

A Hop, Skip, and a Jump:
Your Own Leap of Faith

I can't offer you guarantees; no one can. Life is not a straight path and there are no billboards along the way shouting out what, exactly, your passion is going to be or where you should stop and turn off to get started living it.

Sometimes you just have to take that leap of faith—countermeasured by calculated risk—and go for it. You have to inch away from your comfort zone and embrace those things that might feel uncertain and unproven, to test them for yourself. The good news is, you don't have to jump out of a plane to take your leap of faith. I've taken many leaps of faith in my day, but I've always made sure that the risks were calculated so that, if I did fail, I wouldn't be flattened! But you do have to jump at some point, and the best you can do is prepare, prepare, and prepare some more so that you have an adequate launch pad for that leap.

A leap of faith can be as small as signing up for a class, meeting your mentor for a cup of coffee, or attending a seminar for new inventors. Life is not the movies, and you don't have to bet the farm or risk it all on a single roll of the dice. Taking chances isn't about ruining your life, it's about opening yourself up to what's next... but making sure you still have a home to go back to if the opportunity doesn't pay off. That's not planning for failure, that's just being a responsible adult and giving yourself the launching pad to pursue opportunity, but also the safety net to come back to earth if it's not everything you expected.

For example, my cousin worked driving trucks for an overnight courier service but was displaced with the recession, and now she isn't quite sure what to do next. We were talking one day and I asked her about the future and she said she really liked driving. I thought for a minute before asking her, "Is that what you really like or just what you *know* the best?" Remember, *liking* something and *knowing* something are two different things. It all goes back to comfort and discomfort. What are we comfortable with? What makes us uncomfortable? We often talk ourselves into liking something because it's what we know so well and, after all, change is scary. The known is seemingly better than the unknown, even if we don't know enough about the unknown to determine if we'd like it or not!

That's why you have to get purposeful about your passion and do some work. Sit down—actually carve out some time and focus on all this—and make a list of what you're currently doing. Try to list all the things you like about your job, career, position—whatever you want to call it. Now look at that list a second time and circle all those things that you don't necessarily *like*, but *know*. Let's say, similar to my cousin, you drive for a living. You sit down and write a list of things you *like* about the job:

* I get to make my own hours.

* No two days are ever alike.

* I never know who I'll meet on any given day.

* I live right near the cab station.

* I get to work alone.

Now, take another look at your list. Is "I live right near the cab station" really something you *like* about that job, or just something you *know*? Do you really get to work alone? Aren't there always people in the cab with you? It may still sound like a dream job to you after you've completed this list. (In fact, it's sounding pretty appealing to *me* right now!) But if it's not, if your list is full of just the familiar and not necessarily the joyful, likeable, or even interesting, then perhaps it's time to take a leap of faith and find something new.

Again, it doesn't have to be jumping out of a plane with no parachute. My leaps of faith would generally be considered "safe" by much bigger risk-takers, perhaps because I always make sure to hedge my bet with calculated risk. Sometimes taking that leap can mean allocating resources and money to an entrepreneurial venture, or traveling somewhere new to pursue a job opportunity.

I had a colleague who recently gave up his teaching tenure in the States to go to Korea and teach English. That might look like risk to some of us, but he and his family talked about it for months beforehand, weighed the pros and cons, took an exploratory trip, fell in love with the country, and now, two years into his position, they couldn't be happier. His Facebook page is flooded with pictures of their journeys, his students, their projects, the land, and its people. It really is the experience of a lifetime, but not necessarily a traditional or even "safe" bet as most people would consider it. But that's what makes us unique and different. I think risk, and even opportunity, looks different to everyone depending on where they are in their pursuit and what their passion and interest looks like after some careful review.

Some people are comfortable packing up and heading halfway around the world, whereas others shiver at the thought of taking a trip to Disney World; it all depends on you, your risk tolerance, and how important that opportunity is to you.

The right opportunity is like a siren call that some find hard to resist, even if it means getting out of your comfort zone and taking a leap of faith to try that new, untested, unproven, or uncertain thing.

Opportunity Doesn't Knock Just Once; It's a Revolving Door

Many people have what I call the "lottery mentality." They think, "Well, this is my big shot. If this doesn't happen for me, that's it. I'm done, over, stick a fork in me..." Certainly we've all had those "make or break," *Rocky*-movie moments when there is an actual win-or-lose, pass-or-fail, succeed-or-die-trying element to the opportunity.

Think about the ballerina auditioning for a single slot at a prestigious dance school...and the 200 dancers waiting in line behind her. That's a real "make or break" opportunity.

But outside of that dance studio lives and breathes a world full of opportunities for that dancer that don't hinge on her getting into that school. Let's say she dances her heart out but she's just not what the school is looking for, or there were a dozen dancers in front of and behind her who were.

So she leaves with her head down, and on the way bumps into an older gentleman in a stiff suit and bow tie who says, "Excuse me, miss. I couldn't help but notice your performance today. I was really impressed. I have a dance studio of my own, and, well...here's my card. I'd love if you dropped by tomorrow and we could talk about your future." Unfortunately, the ballerina is still so focused on the dance school opportunity, the single chance she's worked so hard for, that she mumbles something to the man, blows him off, and forgets all about the card. She never saw that the man was actually a representative for the Alvin Ailey American Dance Theater!

Who is to say what kinds of opportunities might have been presented to that dancer had she simply been aware of, and open to, other avenues than the one right in front of her. She'll never know, because now that man's business card, and the opportunity it implied, is gone.

That's why I say there isn't just one passion, or one purpose, for us all. Our lives are linked by the passions that fuel us to the next purpose, and the next, and so on. If I had believed my one purpose in life was to work for the LPGA, I might not be where I am today. But I believe it was working for the LPGA that gave me the tools, awareness, contacts, and expertise to meet the opportunity of working in professional basketball at just the right time.

A large part of success, in pursuing what excites you the most, is opening yourself up to opportunities. Far too many people limit themselves strictly to what they know or are familiar with, and prematurely close doors to opportunities that haven't yet presented themselves. Being able to take advantage of opportunity entails a willingness to set oneself free from one's comfort zone, and get exposed to new environments and a new cast of characters in one's personal and professional life. For some, like my colleague in Korea, that means moving geographically. For others, it might be as simple—though not at all simple to them—as conquering shyness or overcoming self-doubt.

Everyone's leap of faith will look different. For some, it might look like a daredevil leap into the Grand Canyon. For others, it might look like tying their shoes and crossing the street! In either case, the feeling is the same: risk taken, opportunity pursued, nothing ventured, nothing gained. And because opportunity is fleeting, we must follow it wherever it leads. And that is rarely a straight line to our passion, or even success.

I have experienced this firsthand: I did not set out to become a sports attorney, but by being willing to try new things and take a chance on interesting opportunities, I discovered a true passion for it. And as with every accomplishment *and* failure in my life, I view it as the current stage—and not necessarily the end—of my journey. I realize that, as a constantly growing individual, my current career path may eventually lead me elsewhere. Where will I be this time tomorrow? This time next year? This time five years from now? I used to think I'd know, for certain, where I'd be at every stage of my life, but now I know differently. Similar to my other life experience, I now embrace this idea of uncertainty, even anxiety, as I continue to write my story.

DO Talk to Strangers: *They Can Hold the Key to Opportunity*

I have always loved to travel. I have a sorority sister who asks me how I'm able to do it. She states that she could not just get up and go as quickly as I do, citing family, not knowing people in new places, not knowing how to get around, and so on. So it's more so of a fear thing for her. I tell this sorority sister of mine not to think about everything that might go wrong when traveling, but to think of the things that might go right. More than that, I tell her to boil it down to one positive thing to focus on. For me, it is about meeting people! I always end up meeting new people wherever I go, because I make it a point to go new places and talk to people. I don't hide in my room or apartment and stick to myself.

Again, you can't let opportunity—or people—come to you. Sometimes they will, but mostly it's about going to them.

I usually move places where I don't know anyone. Not *just* because I love to meet new people—I could do that in the park around the corner from my house—but because I'm following an opportunity. Usually a great opportunity. It comes back to not waiting but going out and pursuing fortune instead. The best opportunities for you, even the most personal opportunities for you, may not necessarily be around the corner from where you live. This can be a real groundbreaker for some. Many people assume that the only place to look for opportunity is right outside their door. But imagine a world where that dream job, dream passion, or even dream person isn't down the street or around the block but around the country, even around the world!

Luckily, we live in a time and space where connecting with people is pretty easy. You can get on planes or mass transit, which is easy and plentiful, and of course there's the Internet, with programs such as Skype. There are just a ton of new ways in this day and age to connect with people—your friends, family, prospective employees, partners, or other dreamers—in lots of other places. And in my experience, new people mean new opportunities.

I think we have to take a minute and to say, "I'm generally a friendly person; I just have to go out and leave my house and meet some folks." The minute you do, you'll find your social niche—a place where you fit in and can talk openly and honestly with like-minded people about what they do, how they do it, and how you can too.

It's easy to shrink into our own worlds, isolate ourselves, and think we can do it by ourselves. But remember what I said earlier: don't reinvent the wheel every time you want to go for a weekend drive! There are people, maybe not right next door but anywhere in the world, who, with a simple tip, quiet conversation, or just a suggestion, can set your entire life on a different path. The problem with isolating ourselves or waiting for opportunities to come to us is that we can no longer be objective about ourselves, our situations, or our potential.

Look at my cousin: does she *like* driving or does she just *know* driving? What if she just *knows* it and is unsatisfied with just driving, and decides to explore something new, uncertain, or even unproven? She might take a leap of faith and fail, but at least now she knows what she likes—or doesn't like—and can pursue the path that is right for her, rather than the one she just *knows* and is comfortable with.

If we want to find, discover, and pursue our passion, I believe we have to be up for a little discomfort at times. Case in point: I did not think I would be a sports lawyer because my very limited exposure to sports lawyers in college was through the agency side, and I worked more on the entertainment side. The turning point was less about the sport and more about the actual work and the dynamic of the profession, including who I met, the talented people I worked with, and the vibe and environment I worked in.

I don't classify myself as "just" a sports lawyer, or "just" in sports or "just" a lawyer. Instead, I consider that I'm a subject-matter expert who works in sports just as do other subject-matter experts. There are tons of subject-matter experts in every profession; for example, in construction, there are electricians, risk managers whose expertise is in insurance, and more. So whereas folks who work in sports may be sports enthusiasts to some degree, that is not necessarily what led them to that particular career at that particular place and time.

Everyone's motivation and interest is different. It is all about recognizing what does it for you and working from there to craft a passion, a career, and a life. For me, it wasn't about sports first but about the position and the opportunities first, and they just happened to be in sports. When I was with the LPGA, it was more about my expertise in the subject matter and opportunity— trademark and licensing, leveraging intellectual property, event management, retail, and so on—because that was really the bread and butter for the LPGA.

Meet *Clarence Nesbitt*

Clarence Nesbitt is Sports Marketing Counsel for none other than Nike, one of the world's most recognizable brands, so he's someone who definitely knows about following his passion and seeing it through to the very top levels of success. But one doesn't reach the upper ranks at Nike without years of commitment, service, and passion-sparking. In fact, many years of networking within Nike and developing a robust knowledge of the business of sport as well as general sports knowledge helped Clarence get to his current position, where his responsibilities include drafting and negotiating endorsement agreements with athletes, clubs, and federations across Europe. These endorsement agreements have a varying degree of complexity and can include large commercial business relationships.

When I sat down to ask Clarence about his passion, his answer was both passionate and unequivocal: "My passion is basketball," he said enthusiastically, "and it has been that way since the age of 13. I dreamed of becoming an NBA player, but I realized in high school that my academic gifts far exceeded my athletic ones."

While Clarence found himself at a career crossroads, his clarity of vision was such that he could see past his disappointment, and turn a strength into an asset. He explains: "I decided that I would find a profession that allowed me to stay close to the sport that I loved so dearly. To be proficient, I needed to become a good technical lawyer and also to learn about all of the major global sports so I know what the industry practices are. Nike is one of the few places that gives one such an opportunity."

When it came to working for Nike, it seemed like a no-brainer. "I have worn Nike footwear religiously to play basketball since the age of 13," says Clarence, "so it was an added bonus that I was a fan of the brand."

Just as important as his familiarity with the Nike brand, Clarence knew himself, the strength of the passion, and the true direction of his course. "The decision was an easy one," he claims. "You can never make a mistake by following your passion, and this is what I did by accepting a position with Nike five years ago. I have moved twice to be with Nike and it has been an exhilarating ride."

Clarence reflects on what might have happened to, and in, his life if he hadn't made the decision to move and follow opportunity within the Nike organization. "Working in sports at a global level never would have happened without Nike. Most sports organizations only allow for one to get, at best, a national perspective on sport, but today I work on a continental level with football, basketball, track and field, rugby, and action sports."

What's more, Clarence found that moving to follow his passion actually made him more passionate, not just about his work but also about his life, and the world we all live in. "Additionally," he explains, "I have the opportunity to live in a foreign country, which is an extraordinary opportunity given the economic environment in the United States. Moving overseas really expands your horizons on the culture of business as well as working in a multi-national corporation away from the headquarters."

Clarence describes his passionate pursuit of his work less as a leap of faith, and more as a personal journey begun by his parents before him. "I am the child of Caribbean immigrants," he says, "so I am only walking the same path that my parents walked before me. I have used their experiences as my strength during the difficult times. Professionally, it was not so hard because I have remained with the same company, so my day-to-day office life is not so different."

Ultimately, Clarence insists, following his passion has far exceeded his original goals, and helped him evolve both personally and professionally. "I have done things with my professional career that I never dreamed I would achieve. Additionally, I have had some amazing travel experiences and have had to add more pages to my American passport."

Is Clarence living his passion? I'll let him answer that one: "I am absolutely living my passion. I would like to continue to expand my skills and grow on a daily basis. I recognize that no one is promised a job tomorrow with a company, so I try to absorb as much as I can while I have this one."

Like most passionate people, Clarence has learned that career satisfaction isn't a destination, but a journey. And like so many of us, he continues to move forward, progressing, evolving, adapting, and changing to not only embrace the present, but also plan for the future.

Parting Words

We have to remember that opportunity is all around us. There may not be new job openings every day, but if you simply look around at your life situation—where you live, who you know, what you're already doing—you

WILL see opportunities in the form of experiences that will change you, and connections that may lift you to that higher level.

As I said earlier, opportunity doesn't just knock once in your life; it's a revolving door that is always swinging open and inviting you in, if only you'll peer inside and take that leap of faith forward to try new things, even if they're uncertain or uncomfortable. And even if they are, don't worry: in the next chapter, we're going to give you strategies you can use to take along a parachute to cushion your landing if, in fact, you should fall on your face while pursuing that next great opportunity.

Chapter 6

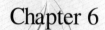

You Don't Need a Parachute to Skydive...You Need a Parachute to Skydive Twice

All passion-sparking includes some kind of risk, but in this chapter I want to discuss how to temper that risk with a specific plan or strategy that ensures you are making your best, most concerted effort toward success. I call it your "parachute," and it's a simple way to mitigate the risk of any opportunity by planning for it, around it, and through it, in case of unexpected challenges or obstacles.

For example, let's say a Midwestern girl wants to move across the country to Los Angeles to be an actress. She's been in some high-school productions, maybe acted in local theater, she's pretty and talented and everyone tells her to pursue her dream. Plus, it's been a passion of hers since childhood, so she decides one day to bite the bullet and make it happen.

Great! Good for her! That's a fairly common risk that can be tempered with just a little careful planning so that she has a "parachute" to cushion her landing if she fails. But before any plan I recommend some careful soul-searching and intense question-asking. What kinds of questions? The types of questions our aspiring actress should ask herself include:

* Do you have a strategy for how to make money until your big break?

* Do you have a budget for living expenses?

* Have you mapped out, ahead of time, where you will live?

* How will you network to find out about auditions?

* Are you willing to put several years into the process of earning your big break?

We can all appreciate the romantic notion of hopping on a bus to LA with nothing but $20 in our pockets and a pack on our back, but the reality is that adult life requires a little—even a lot—more careful planning than that.

So in our starlet's case, these questions may not be fun, sexy, or glamorous—and none of them actually have anything to do with her true passion, acting—but they are necessary for getting (and staying) on the path to achieving her goal. Having an apartment in place, two months' rent paid for, a part-time night job lined up, and friends to network with allows our young starlet to not have to worry about all that once she gets to L.A., so she can put her mind, energy, and focus to going on auditions and pursuing her dream.

So, yes, question-answering and plan-making may not be sexy, but having a strategy in place—and a parachute that will open before crash-landing—is mission-critical for living Life at the Speed of Passion!

It's All Connected

What many people forget on their road to purpose is that it's all connected: even the little things you do to focus on your dreams or pursue your goals have a big impact at some point. I know the decisions I've made along the way often came back to pay off at a later date—even months and years later. Even if something seems trivial, such as a chance meeting or a temp job or a connection you make at this convention or that seminar, everything relates to everything else. You can never write off people or experiences as being a waste of your time if they give you the little pieces you need to put together the whole puzzle.

It's the same as saying, "You are where you're supposed to be." It's easy to get anxious about our careers and current level of success. Everyone else seems to be doing so well, we feel that we're not where we're supposed to be yet, and things are happening too slowly. Yet when you put your life in perspective, you can breathe a little easier knowing that what you're doing at the moment, even if it seems trivial or insignificant, will ultimately have an effect on your future life and career.

One reason I chose to talk about passion and purpose in this book as opposed to strictly "success" is that everyone defines success differently. Many equate the word with a monetary figure, and others identify success with the idea of reaching their own completeness.

What makes you complete, whole, or satisfied with your life? What is missing that you want to achieve in order to feel whole or complete? It's different for each of us. For some of us, we won't feel complete until we travel the world. So that impacts how we live our life, the choices we make, and the opportunities we pursue (such as working abroad, serving in the military, or working for the United Nations). Some of us simply want to pursue our natural talents, abilities, or creativity, regardless of the income we make from that. So we sing in a folk group or in our church choir, or paint murals on schools and community centers. Still others simply won't be satisfied—or complete—until they have that 12-room mansion on the hill with a luxury car in each garage.

There is no right or wrong when it comes to your goals, dreams, desires, passion, or purpose, but you must be open, honest, and purposeful with yourself about what makes you happy, and give yourself permission to pursue that goal, dream, or desire. My definition of success is simply having the ability to explore new things and to create the lifestyle that I want, for myself and for my family. But I acknowledge that at different times in my life success has looked different for me. Success to me is less about what I can "get" or "have" or "own" and more about the freedom and opportunity to try new things that are of interest to me. I believe as we get older, time becomes as important as money, and we make certain allowances for both, each according to our needs, wants, and desires.

Always Plan in Pencil, Never in Stone

Plans are important, but only if you recognize that they are subject to change! So many of us make a plan and, if one tiny thing goes wrong, or our timetable gets delayed, or life interrupts it, we chuck the whole thing rather than simply erasing a milestone, deadline, or due date and amending the plan.

It is never enough to simply follow a path that you may have charted years ago because, as you continue to learn and grow, your desires and interests may do a

180-degree turn and surprise you right into a new passion, plan, or even purpose.

Despite all of the accomplishments I have achieved, some people will ask me, "Are you happy with where you are? Or are there still professional things you'd like to achieve? What are they?" In fact, one of my mentors asked me this just last week. My response was, "Yes, I'm happy, but this isn't my sunset. Did I mention that I want to be a Commissioner, model, and fashion designer—in no particular order?"

I think it's important to ask ourselves these questions every year or so to ensure that we're putting our efforts where they'll yield the most reward. I do believe there are times in our lives when we *are* happy with the state of our professional life, and although I'm not a fan of "coasting" (I believe we should all be learning every day), there are times when we seek professional credibility and respect less intensely. For example, today I feel I have reached a certain level where, rather than worrying about what's next, I can worry about what's "now." That wasn't always the case. When I was at my first law firm, I realized I didn't want to grow in that environment anymore. I still wanted to grow my skillset and become an expert in my area of practice, so I got in touch with the attorney who had recruited me to the firm. She had actually left the firm two months after I started, but we stayed (and continue to stay) in touch. We had a discussion, almost starting from scratch, in which she asked me in what role I saw myself at a potential new firm.

It was a weird discussion to have, because the goal of nearly any new lawyer is to become partner, but during the review process I could better determine where I *did* see myself so to make sure that I would be moving in the direction I needed to go. At that time, I said I didn't see myself becoming a partner. Just saying the words out loud helped me to work through some of the reasons why I wasn't happy in my position. For all my planning and strategizing up to that point, I had never really asked myself if I had the constitution or personality type to actually practice courtroom law. It was only later, once I'd worked at an actual law firm for a while, that I began struggling with the position and my own lack of question-asking. That's why now, even before I make the smallest decision, I run through a series of questions to ensure that it's the right one for me.

There have been other times when I wasn't necessarily in the right position for me at the time, but being in that position helped me connect with folks who would help me later on. For instance, when I was working on strategic plans to grow the retailing licensing business at the LPGA, I talked to a big retailer about running a business unit. I realized I really liked working in a business unit, and this led me to have the confidence to gather more skills to run my business in an entrepreneurial manner. At the time, I had no idea that simple discussion would help me in my own business with my husband, Ken. I certainly didn't know at the law firm that I would do extremely well in running a business unit.

So everything kind of relates to everyone else, and it is about having the confidence to step up and try it.

It's also important to be open to new ideas and, as I always say, meeting new people. I didn't do this alone, nor did I start from scratch. I've worked with, met, or connected with people on nearly every job who helped shape my thinking. This is why you should not live your life as if it was already written out in a script. Sticking too closely to the script is a recipe for major disappointment and will not allow you to consistently align your life with your passions.

The 5 Dangers of Sticking Too Closely to Your Script

There's a certain type of person who often comes to me and says he or she wants to be a sports lawyer. I know from the way this person questions me that he or she is myopic about that particular role, and only wants to work for the NBA, NFL, or MLB. So, if you don't get your dream job on the first application, is that it for you? It shouldn't be. Wanting to be a sports lawyer could mean a lot of things, and there are a myriad of other professional sports leagues or associations, as well as collegiate sports and amateur sports, just to name a few. There are so many opportunities under that "sports" umbrella beyond managing a pro sports team, and the issues are generally the same with other sports groups at a higher level. Use your time on any job to grow and prepare and groom yourself for the next opportunity.

We have to get a little creative sometimes to figure out what it is we want to do. I've always wanted to try things out for myself, regardless of the challenges, obstacles, or minor discomforts. For example, as I mentioned in Chapter 1, I had the opportunity to work as a law clerk at Black Entertainment Television (BET) my last year of law school, and it was an opportunity I really wanted to pursue, so I had to figure out how I was going to live in Washington, D.C, while still in law school, in about six weeks. That meant I had to figure out how to get academic credit, how I was going to eat every day, and where I was going to live while I was there.

No one had ever pursued anything like this at my school before, so this clerkship wasn't an approved program. However, it was unpaid, so I had to receive academic credit for it in order to participate. So, on top of everything else I needed to arrange, I had to fight to convince my school that the credit was valid toward my degree. I could have easily given up if I took "no" at face value, but the opportunity was important to me so I moved heaven and earth to pursue it. Was it in my plan? Certainly not, but it was an important amendment to my plan. When I look at the "strategy" I lay out to reach a goal, it isn't about carving a plan in stone but about having a broader view, being creative, and taking advantage of things as they present themselves, even if it's not in the original plan, strategy, schedule, or timetable.

The job was a great opportunity, and it certainly paid off as I got great exposure from the clerkship and met so many wonderful people with whom I still connect and network to this day.

Enough about me. What about you? Are you in danger of sticking too closely to your plan? Do you think too narrowly and miss opportunities simply because they don't fit in your spreadsheet or matrix? If so, think about these dangers, or costs, associated with sticking too closely to your script:

1. **North, south, east, and west, all roads lead to Rome.** If you think there is only one way to attain your goals, you are sticking too closely to the script. There are many roads to travel, and, eventually, they all lead to where you're supposed to be (even if it doesn't feel like it at the time). I think we've all been in situations that felt rough, or uncertain, or even like a bad fit at the time, but after a few days or weeks we developed a more objective perception and realized that if we simply opened ourselves up to the opportunity, be it to grow our skillset or make new connections, we could make the best of it.

2. **The world isn't necessarily playing by the rules in your book.** There are so many things we can't control, from people to economic conditions to the leadership at our companies. We can't be so rigid that our entire plans get thrown off

track if we get downsized, rearranged, shipped out, or let go. The same goes for the flip side of the coin, if a great experience, class, connection, or other opportunity presents itself.

3. **Creativity counts.** Our journeys don't follow a straight path. Mine certainly hasn't! So we have to get creative to work around our roadblocks, detours, and challenges as they present themselves. A rigid strategy, or script, can prevent us from being open to new opportunities, or even solutions.

4. **Savor the surprises.** As much as I preach a strong strategy, I also relish a good, honest surprise now and again! Surprises are good for us, particularly when they help refresh our perspective or spice up our skillset, and to close yourself off to them is also to say "no" to opportunity.

5. **Success rarely happens in a vacuum.** If you are operating in a vacuum, and never talk to anyone outside of that vacuum, you are severely limiting yourself because you only know what you know. True success, or satisfaction, is about learning from other peoples' experiences and letting them color and inform your own.

One person who knows the value of a plan, as well as the prospect of a great opportunity, is my good friend Marcia Narine.

Meet *Marcia Narine*

Marcia Narine is a Harvard law graduate. She is the former Deputy General Counsel and Chief Compliance Officer for Ryder Corporation. In her work with this international corporation, Marcia oversaw government relations matters, and was (and continues to be) highly sought-after for her expertise. She testified on Capitol Hill many times, and frequently traveled internationally. Although wildly successful by societal standards, Marcia realized that whereas she liked what she did, her true calling in life was to teach others, and she finally caved in to her desire to become a law school professor.

That realization was the "spark" she needed, but it was her subsequent actions in transitioning that made it possible for her to create her "parachute."

Despite challenges like frequent moves with her son and qualifications that were corporate rather than academic, Marcia started off by applying for fellowships. Additionally, she negotiated a year-long consulting arrangement as a part of her exit from her position at Ryder. That was ultimately a win for both her and Ryder as it helped them transition someone else into the role while continuing to utilize Marcia as a resource, and it helped Marcia to maintain a revenue stream while she leapt into the world of academia. Marcia also structured her investments so that it would not be such a huge hit financially before she transitioned to full-time teaching work. It was the combination of these things that became the parachute to help buffer her from any risk. Marcia was then willing to "skydive" into a full-time life as a law school professor because she knew it was possible to move toward her passion.

Like all our journeys, Marcia's path was neither straight nor narrow. Says Marcia, "I've been practicing law since 1992 when I graduated, and the first time I thought I wanted to become a law professor was in 1997. I was going to teach an adjunct class at a local university, called Privacy in the Law...and no one signed up for it! At the time, I was really demoralized." But Marcia didn't let the setback derail her plans. She temporarily put aside the idea of teaching and continued her work at a law firm. But she still had the idea to teach, to inspire law students and give them some practical, real-world knowledge, as well as some solid background in law theory.

Marcia continued at the law firm before going in-house to a Fortune 500 company and did quite well there, gaining increasing levels of responsibility. "I started out as a labor and employment lawyer," she explains, "then I went to be a head of HR for one of the divisions, then I became the compliance and ethics officer for the company, the chief privacy officer, and a deputy general counsel." Between her base salary and annual bonuses, Marcia's income essentially quadrupled. This was important to her because she was about to establish a "Forget You Fund." Marcia didn't want to be like so many other lawyers she knew who lived the kind of lifestyle they couldn't sustain if they wanted to leave the practice to explore other opportunities. Marcia worked hard but had other plans, and wanted to leave herself some financial flexibility to explore them by living below her means and building her Forget You Fund. At some point, the things she enjoyed the most about doing her job, which was developing compliance training, researching the laws of different jurisdictions, lobbying, and public policy aspects, began to push her toward teaching again.

When Marcia reached a personal and professional crossroads, she made the decision to go out and get the requirements she needed to enter the world of academia. According to several well-connected friends who were already law professors, Marcia was about to face some stiff challenges. She recounts, "They all told me, 'It is impossible for you to get a job. You're well over two to three years out of law school. You haven't written any "Law Review" articles, and, other than the fact that you went to Harvard and you're a black female, you have basically nothing to offer in the academic world, and that's just the way it is."

Marcia was shocked. She had an incredible pedigree, had literally testified before Congress on business issues, had repeatedly met with the SEC, and was successful as an officer and attorney for an international company, yet none of that, according to her practical law professor friends, was going to be helpful to her career in academia.

Instead of giving up right there, in 2011 Marcia made the decision to quit her job for one year so that she could write several "Law Review" articles and try to build her academic CV. She also applied for a teaching fellowship at the University of Missouri in Kansas City, even though she had no publications yet, and was accepted. "For these two-year teaching fellowships," she explains, "which are now almost a prerequisite to get a teaching job, they teach you how to teach, and they help you write, and they help mentor you. So, I did that for two years, which meant I had to uproot my son, who was in high school in Miami, and at a place that he very much enjoyed, taking him from the only place he'd ever known. I sold my house because I wasn't sure if I'd be getting back, because after the two-year teaching fellowship there was absolutely no guarantee I would get another job anyplace else."

Marcia credits Judge Marcia Cooke, a federal judge in Miami, with whom she frequently spoke on various panels throughout their careers, for teaching her that sometimes we have to chase what we're interested in, even if it's nowhere close to where we live. A few months before making her fateful decision, Marcia listened to Judge Cooke tell students at a panel, "You might have to pick yourself up and move to one of those square states in the middle of the country to get what you want." Turns out, that's exactly what Marcia had to do for herself!

This was where Marcia's Forget You Fund came in very handy. She explains, "My lawyer friends all thought this move was great. All of them said, 'I would do anything if I could quit my job.' And the number-one thing they said is, "I could never afford to do that financially.' And that's why having that fund was so important."

Marcia took a risk, but it was calculated. Yes, she quit an influential and high-paying corporate job. Yes, she moved to the middle of the country, where she didn't know anyone, from sunny Miami. And yes, she was traveling into uncertain territory. But she had weighed the pros and cons, consulted her long-term strategy, and realized that even if the risk failed, she had a parachute that would prevent a fall from being disastrous.

I don't want to mislead you to believe it was all roses and tiramisu for Marcia—it wasn't. In fact, Marcia lost money for the length of that two year fellowship. But despite the loss, she told herself, "There is a purpose for all this."

After her fellowship, Marcia wanted to return to Miami, to her family and her son's friends. But at every turn, she was told, "It's not likely you're gonna be able to get a job back in Miami. There are 12 law schools in Florida; four of them are in South Florida, and these jobs are competitive. It doesn't matter how the school is ranked. You've got to meet all these criteria..." Luckily, Marcia had written her two "Law Review" articles by this time. What's more, she had taught for two years by the time she went on the market as a law school pro-fessor. She hadn't just taught but had treated the two-year fellowship like anything else she had done: "I treated it like I was applying for a job," she explains. "So everything I did, I made sure to do with excellence. I volunteered for committees. I was invited to speak on panels around the country, notwithstanding my newness to academia. And I got very high ratings on my teacher evaluations from the students. And so they ended up breaking the protocol and offering me a tenured track position at University of Missouri." The job offer offset some of the risk, but it didn't stop Marcia from putting out feelers in larger markets, ultimately resulting in a job offer from St. Thomas in her hometown of Miami, Florida.

Marcia definitely had a plan, and she went about working her strategy year after year. Through ups and downs and obstacles, she pressed forward and kept her options open. And now all that planning and strategizing is really paying dividends. Similar to many who have found their passion, Marcia knew the parameters of her definition of success, and money wasn't always a principle factor. She explains, "You have to always know what the ultimate goal is, and for me, making money was never the ultimate goal. But for some people, making money is the goal. And you have to plan accordingly for that. If making money is the goal, then you're going to do totally different things than someone like me."

Marcia warns of sticking too closely to the script, and challenges all of us to stay open to opportunity...even if it doesn't look like the game plan you created for yourself. "If I had gone and become a professor in 1997 when I first wanted to," she cautions, "or done the adjunct thing and then gone straight to academia, I would not be nearly the professor I think I am today." She adds, "I'm still learning. I could have continued to try, and said, 'Okay, I'm gonna make up a course that everybody will take, like a simple law seminar.' That would have been the easy thing to do, and I would have had my foot in the door. I probably would've been able get some kind of position eventually. But that extra 12 or 13 years gave me more tools, more visibility, more expertise, etc. So, sometimes, the plan doesn't go according to plan, but it's because there's something better for you."

Marcia recounts how her "worst laid" plans helped prepare her for a "best laid" life. She recounts how she thought of quitting to become a plaintiff lawyer: "I remember once going to a Harvard reunion and a woman said, 'You can't leave because you are Deputy General Council of Black females; there's not that many of you. Somebody needs to be there to give women the work and give our black people the work and give the other associates the work.' So, sometimes it's going to be a comment from somebody that's going to really have the ability to change your life and you need to listen to that."

Because of feedback from others, Marcia recalibrated her course and plotted a new one, in a completely different direction. She recalls, "I stayed in-house partly because of those kinds of comments, and then a week later, my boss said, 'I'd like you to start the company's compliance and ethics program.' I told her, 'I'm thinking of leaving...I'm not sure if that's what I want.' She said, 'Stay, and this is what you can do...' And that course of events would not have happened otherwise."

Marcia later recalibrated her course trajectory once again, in accordance with events in the outside world. The world was changing—its politics, its economy, and, in particular, its job market for new college graduates. "I started to ask myself, 'How do I help the students? How do I help students in a terrible job market? And I wouldn't have known all of those things had I become a professor in 1997 because I would have become a traditional, ivory-tower professor without a whole lot of work experience, who still focuses on academic pursuits and doesn't have enough of a foothold in the real world."

That real-world experience has made Marcia the educator and passion-pursuer she is today. Marcia learned, perhaps the hard way, that once you figure out your passion—or even just what excites or moves you—it doesn't have to be passion for the rest of your life. It can instead become a guiding point to set your travels by.

Picture your passion as a lighthouse, leading you on through dark, troubled, or simply foggy times. You can follow many courses to arrive at your destination, and the more courses you take, the better prepared you are to fulfill your ultimate destiny. Without a passion, we often find ourselves traveling around in circles, lost in the dark. But with a passion, no matter how far we stray from our original course, there is always that beacon of light, that lighthouse, reminding us of our true course in life.

You can certainly have a plan and aim for that straight line toward your goal, but just know that life may have other plans for you, so be willing to deviate from that plan to take advantage of opportunities that, at the time, may in fact look like obstacles.

Marcia adds, "You never know where the advice is going to come from. So, sitting around that table and having these people who were saying, 'You can't leave,'" that resonated with me because I realized, 'Wow, I do have a lot of power as an in-house deputy general counsel for Fortune 500 with companies in 12 countries around the world...I have the ability to affect a lot of different lives.' Now my boss is giving me the opportunity to stay and learn a whole new skill set. I would have left as an HR person and as a labor employment lawyer, but I would never have had the compliance expertise, I would never have had the chief privacy officer expertise. So listen to your voice, listen to your friends, but also remember that advice can come to you from anywhere, and even in two short sentences; don't ignore it just because it's not coming from your trusted friend or mentor. It might come from somebody who doesn't even know you very well, but who gives you something to think about."

As Marcia points out, it's never too late to change course and steer in another direction, or take the temperature of the air around and listen to what others might have to offer you in form of insight, advice, expertise, experience, or simply another, objective point of view.

So often we get trapped in the tunnel vision of our careers, our courses, and our direction that we avoid pausing to consider our paths, let alone changing course if necessary.

Parting Words

Both Marcia and I have tried to share our circuitous journeys from here to there and back again in the hopes that they reveal the fluid nature, not just of success but of passion, purpose, and that sense of completeness that eludes so many of us.

Don't be concerned with how fast you get there, or even where you are right now. As Marcia pointed out, those dozen or so years she spent struggling with whether to pursue a career in academia, building a name for herself and taking the long way around to her ultimate calling made her who she is today.

Who's to say what kind of professor she might have become if more folks had signed up for that first adjunct class? And who's to say what kind of career I might have had if I had stayed at that original law firm, making partner, and taking the safe, traditional path?

So in summary, have a path, have a plan, and diligently work it, but don't follow your script so closely that you're afraid to improvise when the opportunity presents itself.

Chapter 7

Tales From an Open Mind

I've said repeatedly that my path hasn't been a straight line to success, but even so, when I talk to people about their careers, their purpose, or their passion, it seems nearly everyone believes that if they just do this, that, or the other, they will follow that straight path right to their personal pot of gold.

I'm all for being dogged in my pursuit of a complete, satisfying, and ideal life, but after sustaining a few bumps and bruises along the way I know the dangers of falling victim to tunnel vision. Life has taught me to keep my options open, and to keep an open mind as well.

Most people (and I think particularly young people) build their hopes and dreams on glamour rather than reality. I was at a luncheon not long ago when a young woman approached me and expressed her desire to become a sports lawyer. I'm always eager to help someone reach her own personal next level because I've been helped so many times by benevolent people—or mentors in disguise. When I asked her why she wanted to be in this line of work, the young lady admitted to having a vague and ultimately unrealistic impression about her chosen field. I could tell by her answers, "Meet the best players," "travel with them," and so on, that she didn't get it. At all. Those things may be big parts of the job for other sports lawyers, but they're not in my career. In fact, the only time "cocktails with the athletes" has ever been a part of my job was when I worked in golf and had to intermittently attend hospitality events or awards banquets. Schmoozing certainly was not a main component of my job description.

She didn't seem to realize that being a sports lawyer is not about having cocktails with the players, and that it actually involves a lot of hard work: writing, reading (sometimes not the sexiest subject matter), negotiating (internally and externally), and, when necessary, burning the midnight oil to meet deadlines or address unexpected, urgent issues all come with the territory. In the end, having some experience in that field as well, I suggested that if she was really interested in being a part of sports and mingling with the players and traveling, she might want to look into the operations, athlete-development or -relations, or entertainment sides of the business instead. When we parted ways, I wasn't sure if she was disappointed or relieved by my answer.

Either way, this anecdote is a perfect example of why it is critical for people who have decided to pursue a particular passion of theirs to take the time to research and ask questions in order to reach a clear understanding of the activities involved in their choice prior to engaging in an all-out pursuit of it.

In other words, keep an open mind. Absolutely pursue your passions, but don't do so while wearing a pair of rose-colored glasses. If you do, you'll be surprised—and extremely disappointed—when the reality of reaching your goal doesn't quite match up with the glamour of pursuing it.

Glamour Versus Reality:
A Career Q & A

I have a pretty simple test for any goal you might have. Before rushing headlong into the Hollywood version of your "dream" job, pause, reflect, and ask yourself a few simple, practical, probing questions first (you know my love of questions by now!).

It's easy to get caught up in the hype surrounding a certain job or even industry. TV and movies, books and videos make a lot of grueling jobs seem more than glamorous. Shows like *The Good Wife*, *Suits*, and *Damages* show high-powered lawyers living high-glam lifestyles in giant houses with fancy cars and lots of down time to hop in and out of bed with the most beautiful creatures. But is that the reality of most real-life lawyers?

A good way to find out is to seek out one, three, or five real lawyers and ask them! Don't get sucked into "the nobility of the profession" answers. Ask a real lawyer, in a real firm, in the real world,

* What do you do every day?

* What do you work on every day?

* When do you start?

* When do you finish?

* Do you have downtime or feel like you have time to explore your other interests?

* What do you like about the job?

* What don't you like?

You may be surprised by their answers! And it's not just the legal profession; every profession has its ups, downs, realities, and dirty little secrets. Even the most glamorous professions, such as supermodel, movie star, or big-name musician, are a lot more work than just posing for magazine covers and shopping for mega-mansions in South Beach.

What's more, the more glamorous the position, the more competitive each slot becomes. One of the reasons I try to mentor young and mid-career professionals, particularly in the legal profession, is because at this level the jobs are so competitive and the stakes are so high. By stakes, I mean the time and money they invest in trying to reach that goal.

So ask some more. Drill down deeper to find out,

* What's the job market like?

* Is it very competitive?

* What is the most challenging aspect of the position?

* Would you do something different if you had to start all over again? If so, what?

* What would you recommend to people to help them navigate their career more efficiently?

Remember, life isn't the movies, and most of us have to work many years in our chosen professions to live the lifestyle we seek. Even dream jobs require lots of hard work to make a reality, and then even harder work—for longer periods of time—to build to fruition. Do you want to spend years and years photographing weddings and babies in department stores before you get to be a high-glam fashion photographer? Are you willing to put in that time, energy, and commitment toward seeing your dream become a reality?

Many people will say yes. Many more will say, "Not on your life"—which is fine. The last thing I want anyone to do is give up on a dream that really suits them, but that's what this persistent questioning, seeking, and fact-finding is all about. This way you can drill down to find out if the career will be a good fit for you based upon the answers you get back from these types of questions.

Many, many people rush into life headlong without ever pausing to kick the tires on their chosen profession, passion, or purpose. We spend more time researching a new car, smart phone, laptop, or tablet than we do planning out the work we'll do for the rest of our lives!

The Plan Before the Plan

One thing I talk a lot about when I speak to groups is The Plan Before the Plan. In other words, there is the work you do to achieve your goals, and then there is the work you do before that, backstage, before you ever set one foot on your chosen career path. Asking questions of a proven mentor is one part of The Plan Before the Plan, but there are other pieces to this plan as well:

* **Be the CEO of Your Life.** I rely heavily on leveraging the experience of others—and I urge you to do the same—but we all have to steer our own ship, no matter how big the crew. People who support and help you are the icing; you're the cake! You have to take initiative and ownership

of working for the life you want. You're reading this book so you're on the right path.

* **Use the resources at your disposal.** You have other resources than just the designated mentors at your fingertips. Read biographies of famous people in your field, read "how to become a..." guides on various industries (the Web is filled with these), and find an organization, forum, or Website devoted solely to helping fresh, creative people join the ranks of a particular industry.

* **Be a passion detective.** Do your Q&As with people in the field, watch documentaries about that field, and read books. In the last chapter we saw how mega-success Marcia Narine treated a simple two-year fellowship as if it was the job application of a lifetime, doing everything with excellence and then some. Treat the Plan Before the Plan the same way; effective planning always makes for a smoother ride to success, if not exactly a straight line!

* **Use purposeful networking.** If you are seeking a mentor to help guide you into your chosen profession, or to help you find a place in that industry, you know people who know people. Say you want to speak to the head of a department, a company's CEO, or even a celebrity. How do you do that? You have to get to those people through the resources you have. Do a little research on

LinkedIn and in online magazines, for example. Reach out and call people, and follow up with e-mails as well: "I know you are super busy but I would so appreciate your reply back when you get the chance," or something to that extent. Go to different mingling/networking events. Go to professional events and speaking panels. Call in and volunteer your time to those events as well. You should also ask people you know if they know anyone you can talk to. How often people overlook this is amazing to me! Even in my own family. At my family reunion, a younger cousin, who is currently in college, mentioned that she wanted to explore dentistry but was shying away from it because she didn't know any dentists and there aren't any in our family. I shared with her that we all go to dentists for care, and that my husband and I have good friends in our social circle who are dentists and could help her get a better understanding of the profession. Try to identify resources by talking about what you want to know and to whom you'd like to talk, even if those folks aren't in your immediate social circles.

* **Stay current on your "Entitlitis" vaccine.** I'm a big proponent of using words appropriately. To give you some idea, I encourage my daughter—who is a whopping nine months old—to use her words, rather than screams and grunts, so

that I understand her meaning. Hilarious? Probably—at least my mother and husband think so. But I figure it doesn't hurt to start early! I say that to emphasize how important it is that I'm using "entitlitis," as it's not a real word. (I didn't make it up; I actually think I co-opted it from my friend and current boss.) Entitlitis is an affliction in which the sufferer thinks the world or other people owe him or her success, status, lots of money, or something beyond an equal opportunity, without actually having to earn it. Your Plan Before the Plan should include healthy and regular vaccinations to ward off entitlitis so you don't start to feel that anyone owes it to you to talk to you or help you. Should they? It depends on which side of this fence you sit. Do they have to? Absolutely not. Asking questions of people, and getting honest answers, is a privilege, not a right, so appreciate it when it does happen.

With each step you are coming closer to someone who can help you make your dream a reality, and as you peel back each layer of your chosen profession, you can see how it really works—and determine if you want in or out!

Don't Just Be a Writer,
Be a Rewriter

If writing this book has taught me anything, it's that lots of magic happens when you're writing the rough draft, but a lot more happens in the rewriting phase. Life, I feel, is much the same.

We all write a script for ourselves, either intentionally or unintentionally. That script starts from early on, even in childhood, when we first decide to grow up to be a ballerina, fireman, politician, doctor, lawyer, or even a princess.

Some of us keep writing the same script despite the changes in our life and the realities of that chosen profession. How many little girls still strive to be a princess, even if it's just reality TV "royalty?" But if you're serious about yourself, your purpose, and your passion, you'll learn to rewrite your script, continually, with each new piece of information.

In an earlier chapter we talked about a young girl from the Midwest who picked up stakes to go to L.A. and become an actress. Let's call her Jasmine. I had some advice for Jasmine in that earlier chapter, but now let's see how she's doing. Maybe Jasmine has been on a few auditions, gotten a bit part or two, maybe played an extra, and realized that finding success in her chosen profession isn't exactly the way the Disney Channel portrays it. She's learned some life lessons, and although she didn't have a Plan Before the Plan, she's making one now.

Why? Because she's been bitten by the entertainment bug, and is rewriting her script. She's learned that being an actress isn't necessarily her strong suit. Yes, she can do it, but she's much better suited to a life behind the scenes. In fact, she's taken her eye for detail—something she never realized she had before—and put it to use in the scheduling department at a small production company. Now, instead of acting in front of the cameras, she plays a big part behind the scenes making sure that the actors have everything they need to succeed. Every day Jasmine pays attention to the details to ensure that the lighting guys are all on time, the equipment they need is on the scene, it's all on budget, and everybody has a role to play and a time card to punch.

Her business savvy has helped her carve out a place for herself in a highly competitive, highly sought-after profession—the field of entertainment—even if it wasn't necessarily what she came out to L.A. to do. Jasmine has learned that the real magic of her life script came not in just writing down her hopes and dreams, but continually rewriting her script to reflect her current reality and changing spark of passion.

Embracing Life's Detours:
Change = Opportunity

Just as the rest of us will eventually, Jasmine realized that life is full of detours. Some of us stop at the first detour, give up, and settle in. That detour may lead to dropping out of college because it was too hard, or because there weren't enough slots open in the major of our choice. We may be detoured into the first job we can get out of college, or high school, even if it's not our dream job. That detour becomes home base if we're not careful.

But others face a detour and plan accordingly. I went to law school with a girl who really wasn't suited to being a lawyer at all. But that was the script she'd written for herself, and she was dogged in her pursuit of acting it out to the letter. She graduated with a great academic record, found a job...and then realized it wasn't for her. She saw a large law firm as the setting of her own script and, after working tirelessly to get there, she hated it. She quit law and no longer practices. It has been years since we've been in touch, but I often think, maybe if she'd been open to changes in her life script, if she'd rewritten it just a little along the way, amended it to perhaps start out at a smaller firm, or open one of her own, or specialize in a particular niche that better suited her personality, she might still be practicing law. Instead she had her blinders on through endless hours of study, years of law school, all the hard work and effort it takes to get hired and carve out a name, and then...it was all over. A dozen years spent in the tireless pursuit of someone else's script, and now what? She has to start all over again.

Few of us have that kind of time to devote to the wrong passion, especially when we can avoid the process altogether with a little rewriting and a Plan Before the Plan.

That being said, I'd hate to think that my friend's time in law school, and even as a lawyer, was "wasted" time. She was a shy person, at heart, and that doesn't always translate to the legal profession. My hope is that she saw her time in the legal profession as a detour, and used what she learned there to do something else more closely aligned with her own life script.

Hopefully, the rest of us take shorter detours. I've made no secret about my own choices in life, personal or professional, and how some have been right and others wrong. But all have been *my* choices and I made them with the best of intentions. That's why keeping an open mind is so important. When you go into every opportunity realizing that it could succeed or fail, that you could win or lose, you limit yourself. Life is not "pass or fail," it is multiple choice. We all have choices, every day, to take even our biggest failures and turn them into successes.

Jasmine went to Hollywood to be a movie star. Now she's a star, but behind the scenes. She faced a lot of detours along the way, but didn't let those stop her from finding success in a new passion, one that maybe isn't as glamorous or sexy as walking the red carpet of a big movie premiere, but that suits her new script revisions just fine.

We can all take a lesson from her book when it comes to not sticking too closely to our own life script, and to seeing detours not as failures, pit stops, breakdown lanes, or dead ends, but as opportunities to step back, reassess, rewrite, and then move in another, hopefully better direction.

Meet *Yolanda Rabun*

A prime example of this chapter's theme of not limiting ourselves is Yolanda Rabun. She is a full-time lawyer at IBM in North Carolina. I refer to her as my "bundle of energy" idol because I am so inspired by her energy to do amazing things, and I use her spirit to kick my butt in gear when I feel like I'm dragging the ground a bit. Yolanda is also a full-time songstress, actress, wife, and mother of two. She does television commercials and performs in musicals. She has even been on Broadway. Her children also appear in commercials and have written a children's book. As if her plate was not already full, Yolanda formed a jazz group that performs regularly on the East Coast and Southern United States and has toured in Europe twice within the last year and a half.

She does not allow her passions to diminish the quality of work she does during the day as a lawyer for IBM. Rabun somehow finds a way to incorporate aspects of her singing and acting career into her day-to-day life as a lawyer.

Parting Words

A purposeful life requires being open-minded about everything you do. If an opportunity doesn't work out and you see the end is near, take stock and salvage what you can from that opportunity and us it to lead you to the next, and the next, and the next. Remember, as I stated earlier, opportunity doesn't just knock once; it's a revolving door opening over and over again, just for you.

You're the CEO of your life. It's up to you to decide whether you'll take that risk, take another step, or walk through the open door.

Chapter 8

Some People Bring Happiness Wherever They Go, and Others When They Go

Success never happens in a vacuum. As much as we are responsible for our own destiny, none of us ever does it all alone. I have been assisted, in almost every success, by one person or many people who supported me, prepared me for a leg of my journey beforehand, or helped ease my passage during the process. I had to take the steps to success myself, but these friendly, persuasive, nurturing, and often demanding folks were pivotal in helping me move in the right direction.

I believe the same is true for all of us. Much of pursuing our passion is predicated (actively or passively) on our relationships. Other people's willingness to share, counsel, advise, or do anything to help us is based on whether they like us or not, and, quite often, *how* we ask for their help. Again, here is where good ol' fashioned common sense comes into play.

The Two Kinds of People in Your Life: *Happiness-Bringers and Happiness-Takers*

As Jim Rohn, the author of *Exceptional Living*, has been so famously quoted as saying, "You are the average of the five people you spend the most time with." I'd like to qualify that statement by adding that there are two kinds of people in our lives:

1. **Happiness-bringers** are people you like being around. People who are upbeat and positive, whom you feel enhance your day and spirit just by being around them. They walk into the room and you light up because you know they are there to bring happiness, pure and simple.

2. **Happiness-takers** are negative. They are downers and they usually suck the spirit and joy from the room. Everything is a trial or tribulation around them. Rather than build you up, they tear

you down. The type of things they say, and their very attitude affects your mindset in a negative way.

When it comes to exploring new things, to sparking your passion and pursuing your purpose, you need to be around people who support you and facilitate what you need to bring forward.

The 5 Gifts of Happiness

I talk a lot about happiness because it's a part of my definition of success. Early I talked about my idea of success being the freedom to live the lifestyle I choose, and I choose happiness! But I recognize that for many people, success comes first and happiness second.

What a grim way to live. Sometimes, life is dismal, cruel, and harsh, but not *all* the time. I've tried to be happy in all phases of my life, regardless of what I was going through. That's not to say that I'm totally Pollyanna and don't have down times. For sure, I have bad days or even weeks in which I think, "Geez, did I draw the short straw? Because the hits keep coming!" And as a result, I may vent or be a complete grump, or both. (Much to my mother's chagrin, I have the uncanny ability to vent in a manner that could rival a sailor because I appreciate that curse words mean things too.) But at the end of that, I still choose happiness—that is, I choose to say, "XYZ is totally crappy, but things will get better, and I'm going to do ABC to get to that 'better.'"

Many will say, particularly in most business professions, that happiness is a "soft skill," or something that comes after success, or after an achievement, or at the end of a deadline, goal, or systems process. But to my way of thinking, happiness informs, colors, and helps all of the above to be more effective, more successful, and, quite often, more profitable.

I have narrowed this philosophy down to what I call **The 5 Gifts of Happiness**:

1. **Confidence.** I believe that confidence is a direct byproduct of happiness. Think about it: when we are happy, our belief in ourselves is stronger, and with a stronger sense of self comes more and more confidence. Confidence, I believe, is not about being cocky, arrogant, or competitive, but about feeling right, complete, and proud of who we are and what we've achieved, are achieving, or are simply trying to achieve. What's more, confidence and happiness go hand in hand.

2. **Clarity.** "I can see clearly now, the rain is gone." That's a song about happiness, about getting rid of the grey skies in one's life and opening up to the sunshine, blue skies, and white clouds of a free and uncluttered mind. When we lose the clutter, the anxiety, the doubt, and the fear, we can see more clearly, and with clarity comes a more precise and purposeful vision for our own lives.

3. **Decisiveness.** When we have the first two gifts of happiness—confidence and clarity—our minds are less cluttered by insecurity, doubt, and anxiety. When we doubt less, we can make clearer, bolder, even wiser decisions about every area of our life, not just our passion or profession.

4. **Wisdom.** Happiness makes us wise in the real meaning of life. When we discover happiness, we know what's important to us and tend not to sweat the small stuff so much. This is wisdom we could all do with a little more of, don't you think?

5. **Freedom.** There is freedom in happiness. Freedom from doubt, from confusion, from fear and anxiety. I'm not saying that happiness makes you bulletproof—I still worry about things that are both within and outside of my control. However, it absolutely gives you armor against the daily humdrum and grind that drags so many of us down. In that sense, it gives us the freedom to enjoy every step of the journey, not just the fabled finish line.

As you can see, there is a strong case for not putting off happiness another moment. But what happens when others try to rob you of your happiness?

Are You Bringing Happiness, or Taking It?

I am going to tell you a story about bringing happiness that starts with taking it!

I was not always a smooth negotiator. In fact, growing up, I had quite a temper, along with quite a mouth. I was a fierce fighter against injustice. Even today, though I'm more selective about how I deliver the message, I'm still the person who says something when I see a wrong regardless of whether anyone else agrees or not. As an adolescent, I wasn't quite as concerned with delivery and I fought everything that I perceived to be an injustice at every level—including when they came in the form of punishments my poor mother handed out! I remember one time my mouth had gotten me in hot water again, and to punish me, my mother forced me to read *How to Win Friends and Influence People*, by Dale Carnegie, which at the time I viewed as cruel and unusual.

And if that wasn't penalty enough for the young, edgy, and mouthy Eve Wright, I was also ordered to write chapter summaries. The nerve! But writing them made the information stick. The book, and its author, made such an impression on me at the time that I still quote Dale Carnegie to this day, from memory, at the slightest urging.

What I viewed at the time as the "worst punishment ever" actually proved to be a valuable life lesson that I've come to apply on a daily basis in my speaking events and even within the actions of my own life. With her "punishment," my wise mother actually helped me to see that life wasn't always the drudgery I made it out to be, and that yes, in fact, she and Dale Carnegie knew just a little bit more than I did!

It also helped me learn to keep an open mind, not just about right or wrong—as I perceived them at the time—but about happiness-bringing and happiness-giving. From that day forward I began to surround myself with happiness-bringers, and gradually removed happiness-takers from my life. It wasn't always easy.

The Freedom of Letting Go:
Embracing Happiness-Givers and Removing Happiness-Takers

I am not always sunshine and light, and I've been guilty of robbing people of their happiness from time to time, however unintentionally. Part of my job as a lawyer is to think about the worst-case scenario and try to mitigate risk in the event that the worst comes to pass. Sometimes the stakes are low, and sometimes they are high, but either way, it doesn't always make me Mrs. Fuzzy Bunnies and Sunshine. But practice makes perfect, and every day I work hard at what I call "relationship nurturing" and creative resolutions to be productive at what I do. Relationship nurturing is the concept of building on positive relationships (happiness-bringers) and weeding out negative ones (happiness-takers). The first rule of a relationship is that there are two sides: it's not just about what you can get, but what you can bring as well. So you can't be a happiness-taker and expect to be surrounded by happiness-bringers, because, guess what? It's tough to consistently be around a happiness thief. Happiness-bringers are smart folks; they only want to be around other happiness-bringers!

A friendship is not all about you and your needs. The way you deliver information matters; you should be giving as much as you get. I believe the older we get, the more of life we've lived, and the more we've helped others and been helped by others, we come to truly value and appreciate the happiness-bringers in our life. Conversely, happiness-takers only see one side of a relationship: how it affects them. They may act like friends, but only when they can "get" something from a relationship, even if it's just drama or them feeling better by making you feel worse.

Life is short, particularly for passionate, passion-sparking people. We want to live life to the fullest, achieve our goals, embrace our relationships, and live satisfying, complex, "complete" lives, and happiness-takers simply rob us of the energy we need to sustain that kind of lifestyle. So how can you get rid of them? How can you embrace happiness-bringers and squelch the dreaded white noise of happiness-takers? Here are a few tips on how to do just that.

* **Claim it.** You deserve happiness. You deserve the right to bring happiness as much as others de-serve—or think they deserve—the right to take it. When you have happiness-takers in your life (drama queens and crisis addicts and time vam-pires—you know who I'm talking about!), why do you think they deserve more happiness than you? It is not unfair or selfish to demand your own happiness, especially when it's not hurting—but only helping—others. Remember that and it will be easier to let go of the happiness-takers in your life.

* **Weed your garden.** Part of your responsibility as the CEO of your life is to tend to your garden. You don't have to build a fortress around your life overnight to drive the happiness-takers out. Depending on how many you know, it may take some time. That's okay. Give yourself permission to weed the happiness-takers from your life's gar-den, one at a time. Even shutting down one will instantly make your life happier when you imag-ine the happiness they're not taking away from you!

* **Stick to your guns!** One thing we all know about happiness-takers is that, in addition to robbing our ambition, energy, and fun, they are master

manipulators. They will make you feel guilty for cutting them off, not replying to their phone calls or repeated texts, and that's okay! Stick to your guns! Remember, you deserve happiness, and only those who would take it from you will tell you any different!

* **I repeat, you deserve this!** Finally, remember that we often put ourselves last, and to seek our true calling in life, we can't do that any longer. I can't imagine purposefully robbing someone else of his or her happiness, and I imagine if you're reading these words right now, you feel the same. But we allow people to rob our happiness all the time, with their complaints, moaning, groaning, and negative words, thoughts, actions, and energy. Why? Because we feel too guilty to say no, let alone goodbye. That ends now. You deserve happiness and it is not wrong or selfish to say yes to your own happiness and no to those who would take that happiness from you.

You will be amazed at what happens when you are only surrounded by happiness-bringers—you'll inspire, encourage, support, and celebrate one another. It will be like finally tuning a radio: you've been listening to static and white noise and crackling, until finally you stumble upon the right station and dial in the beautiful music you need as the soundtrack to your life's purposeful and passionate journey!

Meet *Elke Suber*

Now we've come to one of my favorite parts of this chapter: allow me to introduce to you my friend and one of my favorite happiness-bringers, Elke Suber. Today Elke is a senior attorney for Microsoft Corporation, and oversees legal support for the worldwide operations of Microsoft's Windows Live (WL) Messenger and its WL Mobile Services business. She speaks regularly on technology, intellectual property, and diversity issues. She has served as a speaker for the National Bar Association, American Bar Association, ALI-ABA, and the Black Entertainment and Sports Law Association (BESLA), among others.

Elke is a career woman as well as a full-time mom. And she is one of those people whose demeanor rarely turns sour. She is a perfect example of the kind of person who brightens up a room simply by being her own happy, genuine self. The way she interacts with people can even change the way other people react to one another, and for that reason she is one of my all-time favorite happiness-bringers!

When I asked Elke how she stays so positive, so strong, and so supportive, so often, she credits it to a basic attitude of gratitude. Happiness, she says, comes from "appreciating what you have versus focusing on what you're lacking. And I think when you start with a gratefulness of what you have in your life, it really makes it easy to have that positive attitude because you're walking with a sense of grace about you." Elke credits her parents, grandparents, and especially her grandmother with instilling her with this sense of grace and gratitude early on. "My grandmother lost her parents at a very young age," Elke explains. "She didn't have a formal education. Yet, she made a way for my mother, her daughter, to come to America to have an opportunity. Being an immigrant from Trinidad, my grandmother always looked at this country as a place where you could come from nothing and be something. That's the quintessential American dream, but she really held onto it."

From a young age, Elke recalls, gratitude was a way of life. "We weren't very well off growing up," she recalls, "but we had a lot of love in our house. And even when we didn't have things, there was still a lot of joy in my family and in how we were raised. And so I think that, having a positive outlook, some of it might be nature, but a lot of it is nurture and how I was raised to focus on the things to be grateful for."

Although Elke is a bonafide happiness-bringer, she's well aware of happiness-takers and the damage they can do to someone's state of mind. Still, she points out, positivity will always win out. "Start everything from a positive place," she suggests. "So even when I'm dealing with difficult people, I remember that everyone shows up to your doorstep with something else that could be going on in the background."

Elke warns that not all happiness-takers set out to be that way, but wind up there perhaps out of frustration or even defeat. She also contends that sometimes, the best way to deal with a happiness-taker is with laughter. "Two people can't have a hot head," she says, "so I try to use humor, and I kind of take a step back and realize that it's not about me. This person might have shown up with a bad attitude because something terrible is happening behind the scenes that I don't know about, so either I put myself in their shoes or at least I step out to not take it as a personal attack on me."

It's this powerful negotiation skill—putting herself in someone else's shoes—that has helped Elke reach the highest levels of law, as counsel for CIGNA and Microsoft. One of Elke's key pieces of advice, happiness-wise, is having a walk-away point. "If I can't help turn the situation around," she explains, "then I leave the situation. So that also helps to minimize damaging the relationship in the event I need it later. So maybe you end a meeting early. You end a conversation early. And maybe the next time you see that person, it's a better situation. And if they turn out to be someone that there really is no getting around to having a decent relationship with them, then that's a relationship I would have to leave alone."

This "walking away" from happiness-takers can be challenging, particularly because so many of us—Elke included—are people-pleasers who want to be liked. But that's the trap we fall into: we're afraid to say no or walk away, because then, what if that person doesn't like us anymore? But with age, and wisdom, comes the realization that we can't be liked by everyone, and that it's more important to like ourselves than cater to the whims of those who would steal our happiness.

Elke warns that if we don't get rid of our happiness-takers, the toll it takes is only on ourselves. "Early in my career," she explains, "I would spend time ruminating on a situation that I had no information about and that really ended up being a waste of my own energy and time. And as I matured, I got better about not spending time concerned or ruminating about someone who's in a negative space. I can only control me. I can't control another person and I may not always be able to control a situation, but I can control how I show up in a situation."

Elke describes how dealing with the negativity of others often robs us of the time, energy, and, above all, passion required to fuel our own dreams. So how does Elke deal with happiness-takers? She shares with us a simple strategy involving teamwork. "I don't do it all on my own," she says. "I have that circle of close, trusted advisors, people I know I can call and say, 'Good Lord, I was just dealing with this person and they were acting the fool, and I almost...' And the biggest advice I always get is to take a day, and step out of the situation. Tell somebody you have to follow up. Because then I have an opportunity to calm down and come back in a better, more positive place."

Elke points out that rather than just a personal passion, her positivity has had professional benefits as well. "I have a reputation for being positive," she confesses. "It has certainly helped me immensely in my career because that means you have to have all the basics, right? Which is...she's smart, she knows what she is doing, she's going to bring value...but she can also get along with people. Then you're somebody people want to have in the room. You're somebody people want to invite into the conversation. And I know I have been blessed in my career to be pulled into conversations or to be put on projects because people said, 'Okay, she's the full package. She's got what she needs from a technical perspective. But I just like working with her because she's easy to work with.' Not because I'm a pushover, not because I'm not gonna give you my view, but that I can do it in a way that is respectful and doesn't turn somebody off. So, I have built a reputation as being a great collaborator and that is something that's so important and critical in business today. But part of being a great collaborator is being able to work with different styles, different personalities, people from different backgrounds without being offensive and still bringing your strengths to the table.

"Being collaborative doesn't mean you get along with everyone or that you fold to everybody else's position. Instead, I know that I have benefited because I have built a reputation as someone who is collaborative and that I can work on a difficult issue without alienating the team around me. And that attitude has led to promotions, special projects, leadership opportunities within the company, and, most recently, to Shanghai."

Humbly as ever, Elke is referring to her new role at Microsoft. She explains, "A year ago I got a new opportunity to help with the expansion of a new business that Microsoft entered into, which is the Microsoft retail stores. These are Microsoft stores where we sell our products, as well as our partner products and accessories. And the big thing that I've had the opportunity to do in this job is actually help with our international expansion into China."

Elke has discovered that her collaborative expertise has helped her not just personally, but also proactively as a team leader. "Where the collaboration piece becomes so important," she explains, "is that I manage a small team. Now, my team is not responsible for getting all the legal work done for the international expansion. I actually have to partner across the department for that, working with employment law specialists, migration law specialists, corporate law and business entity structure specialists, commerce specialists, privacy and data protection specialists, etc., to answer questions like, 'How do we handle payments in China? So as you can see the list becomes a 'V-team' of several different specialist lawyers plus outside counsel that I have to work with and manage. And so being someone who can collaborate, not just within my own team but across the department—to work with lawyers who don't report to me, but on whom I'm dependent to land my project successfully, and to work with lawyers in China (I have specialist lawyers there, both internal to Microsoft and external to Microsoft)—has been key to this role. So has leadership, because I have to ensure that I'm working with folks in a manner that they will be reporting up to me what work they've completed so that I can then talk to my business leaders and help them explain where we are on all of these various legal work streams."

Harmony and happiness aren't the first things you normally think of when it comes to corporate leadership, but when you work in a collaborative environment and lead from a collaborative level, you're not just leading, you're managing up, you're managing laterally, and you're managing down.

So how does Elke factor happiness into the equation? How does that help to keep those folks motivated to continue to move to where she needs them to be? Elke explains, "When you have a number of people who are not direct reports to you, and this isn't their full-time job, the biggest thing to get everyone circled around is a common commitment, or a common mission, of why we're all in this project, and what we are trying to accomplish. So it was important for me to understand what everybody's personal goal was: What do they care about? What's important for their career out of this project? So, for example, if I'm working with the employment lawyer from HR, and she's got a lot of different projects, at the end of the day when she's reporting up to her management structure, what's important for her? What will motivate her to do a great job on this project? I have to make it a win-win in order for folks to want to collaborate with me. I have to appeal to whatever they are interested in."

Discovering her team's common mission, as well as personal motivators, was vital to helping Elke find success. "The two things that I figured out were really key," she explains, "are (1) getting everyone aligned around a common commitment, and then (2), understanding 'What's in it for them?' Once I could understand that, then I could be the cheerleader, when I needed to be, or I could be the person who helps them get recognition in their organizations, if that was appropriate. Because it isn't just about me succeeding; I have to figure out how the entire team can succeed, and that then comes back to, 'What's in it for each of the team members?' That's how I manage to get people excited about what we're doing: because there's something in it for each of them for us to get to this common goal."

Feedback is another part of job performance, and even job happiness. Elke's answer to feedback can best be expressed in three words: "Often, often, often." Why so often? She explains, "Because once you begin a feedback loop, there's just sort of a back and forth on a weekly basis or a regular sync, then people feel like their boss is actually paying attention to the work they're doing. I always provide feedback in a way that it's constructive and not in a way that it is destructive. So what do I mean by that? Say I get something from the court person I'm working with, and it might have been delayed or it wasn't clear to me what the answer was. Now, if I sit on that for two months and then go back to him and say, 'Hey, I really didn't get what I needed and I haven't been able to explain this to my business, and now, it is a fire drill...,' that's not a good situation.

"Instead, if I get advice back from my colleagues, review the advice, then if there is something that I don't understand and if I have feedback on it or I need changes, I can get back to them immediately—and not on an e-mail with a whole bunch of people, but by picking up the phone and having a one-on-one conversation. That has been really helpful, just getting off the e-mail and picking up the phone."

Elke makes a strong point in that half of working with people is the skill of knowing yourself—in other words, self-assessment. You have to know yourself to be yourself, and that's what everyone in business expects, from customers and clients to coworkers, colleagues, and CEOs. They can choose anyone for the job, or to invest in or back; why should they choose you? If you don't know yourself, you'll never be able to answer that question. And if you're so busy trying to please others— to make them happy at the cost of your own happiness, hopes, dreams, and desires—you'll never know yourself, or be able to *be* yourself either. Not only does Elke know herself, but she also knows her role and how it can best help her employers, coworkers, customers, and the world she lives in. But above all that, she is a happiness-bringer extraordinaire, and we can all learn a little something about how much she's accomplished, and how much joy, energy, and enthusiasm she's brought to others along the way.

This brings us to her passion and, more specifically, how she found it. For Elke, it all started with energy. She explains, "You have better energy when you can come to work in a positive place. So for me, figuring out your passion goes back to that energy conversation, and even back to law school. I didn't know anything about law school, I just had this English degree and I was like, 'Well, I wanna be a professional...should I be a professor? Or maybe I'll try this law thing?' Then in law school, I had great teachers around me. Kevin Deasy was one that stands out, and he really encouraged me to take a number of different courses. And by doing that, I basically fell upon two areas that I really was interested in: international trade work and copyright and trademark law. Because I was an English major, I had a patent professor who sort of taught the all-up IP [international property] course. I went to him after the class and I said, 'Wow, I did great in this class...I think I really like this...what would I need to do to get this job?' That professor wasn't exactly very encouraging and sort of shared with me, 'Well, you don't have a technical background...this is really a boutique-type work...it might be really difficult for you.' As a result, I kind of put IP aside. But then I did a federal clerkship and had patent cases and trademark cases and copyright cases and realized, 'Well, wait a minute, the judge doesn't have a technical background, and I am his clerk, assisting him on these cases...' So the spark was ignited again because it didn't feel like work when I was addressing those issues or doing the research. It just felt like fun. But, of course, by that time, I had already taken a job that wasn't an intellectual property job to follow my clerkship, and I got into the job, and I liked the job, but I still felt, 'I really wanna do IP work.' So, one of my strategies to figuring out how to fulfill that passion and to transition into the area was to start taking all of my CLE [Continuing Legal Education] courses in IP law."

Elke had found her passion, and now she needed a plan. In true Elke style, she didn't waste any time: "I joined the local IP bar," she recalls. "I just embedded myself into local IP community, going to their events and learning right through the CLE programs whatever the latest and greatest was. Then I did some pro bono work, so that I could start to get some experience because I wasn't getting it at the firm. And by putting those two or three things together as my strategy, if you will, it led to creating relationships with actual intellectual property lawyers. Lawyers who could say, 'Hey, this position is coming open. And with your litigation background, you might be able to transition into a role.' And that is exactly how I ended up joining the Intellectual Property Group at Akin Gump. I went in using the litigation skills, but I had all of these relationships that helped prepare me for the interview, and I had all of the pro bono work I had done, as well as the CLE courses, so I could speak about the IP issues with the level of confidence because I trained myself."

As Elke points out, the strategy you adopt to pursue your passion may not go in a straight line, but it does move you forward, even if it can sometimes feel like you're only standing still. You have to adopt an attitude of, "I am going to try it, and if I like it, then I'll put a strategy in place for maneuvering into this, and then I'll finally make the jump." But it often won't happen at all if folks don't respect, or even like you enough to say, "Hey, we heard about this, or there might be an opportunity here, or think about exploring this." That kind of alliance-building and networking shortens your learning curve and gets you to your destination sooner.

Parting Words

As Elke reminds us all, "You have to do the work." Happy or unhappy, success or failure, comfort or discomfort, ultimately, it's up to each and every one of us to create our own fortune, good or bad. It's up to us, ultimately, to surround ourselves either with happiness-bringers or happiness-takers. I chose to devote a whole chapter to this concept because I want us all to remember how vital it is to stay happy, or at least positive.

Life won't always work out, our journeys don't follow a straight line, and as successful as we are, there will always be another obstacle around the corner to derail our plans or force us to rewrite our script. Keep going anyway! Rewrite if necessary, recalculate and recalibrate, and keep. Marching. Forward.

Many people will credit your success to "luck," but in my experience—and we've talked about this previously—we make our own luck, much as we make our own happiness. And that good "luck" comes from plenty of preparation—the Plan Before the Plan—and lots and lots of continually changing, evolving, and passionate work. Happiness, too, takes work.

Happiness isn't an illusion, or even a destination; it's a state of mind. You don't have to wait until you have that big house, three-car garage, or even retirement to attain it. In fact, the happier, more positive, and more hopeful you are, the more effective you'll be at turning your dreams into reality. That's because you'll realize that dreams can come true, with a lot of hard work and plenty of positivity along for the ride.

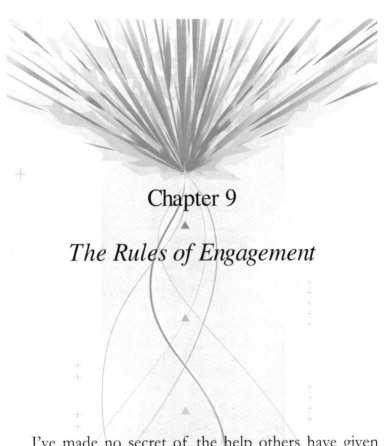

Chapter 9

The Rules of Engagement

I've made no secret of the help others have given me on my own passion-sparking journey. Though I've worked hard and learned mainly through trial and error, feeling my way as I go, I couldn't have done so without the gentle guidance and the opportunities presented by a host of helpful colleagues, coworkers, mentors, and what I call "allies" and "cheerleaders." I've talked about how important these folks are and how to effectively utilize their experience and expertise if they are willing to help you. Now, let's talk about how to go about gaining these allies and cheerleaders: "The Rules of Engagement." In other words, we've seen how important these allies and cheerleaders can be, but...

* How do you go about courting these allies and cheerleaders?

* How can you find the help you need to get where you want to go?

* How do you identify who can introduce you to an opportunity?

* Who can shepherd you along the path to success?

* How do I repay their generosity?

Understanding the importance of finding allies and cheerleaders—both professionally and personally—is one thing, but having the ability to *do* it is something entirely different.

Some people readily engage and connect with people instinctively; this skill is reminiscent of how ducks take to water. However, there are others who really struggle, perhaps due to shyness or lack of confidence. They haven't the foggiest notion of how to initiate and nurture these types of relationships. For them, we have to go back to the playground.

The Importance of Playing Well With Others

Although our time on the playground has long since passed, I believe that embracing what I call the "playground mentality" still works, no matter what your age, income, status, or position.

Think about it: the playground was typically the first place we learned how to interact with others—others who perceived and judged us as having a certain personality. It was a place of influence and a place to be influenced. We often chose our spot, our friends, and our "game of choice" here.

It could be a little intimidating at first, this big open space and all these children with their different toys, clothes, and personalities.

* Should you shuffle to the left, to the right, or wander down the middle?
* Who will accept you?
* Who might help you?
* Who could hurt you?

Instinctively, we made choices in the blink of an eye—some good, some bad, but all educational in helping us learn not only who we were, as individuals, but also how we fit as part of a larger, more influential group. When we found the right fit within a certain group, whether with one tight BFF or several friends who just "got" us, we tended to gain confidence, grow, and blossom in that sheltering place of support and friendship. If we occasionally fell in with the wrong group of friends, we felt it. Our world grew dark for a moment; we didn't feel as influential, powerful, or accepted. We phased out of this group until we clicked somewhere else and were able to shine again.

The fact is, life isn't so different now. What is a workplace but a big playground? We walk in on that first day and we may have an assigned seat/cubicle, but we still have to make our way. We don't want to be the lone wolf, toiling away with no resources, network, or support. Instinctively, we want to find that group that will nurture, guide, and support us. We go left, we go right, we smile and shake hands and listen and interact until we find the right fit, and then...we shine. That's not to say we don't have to depend on our own instincts, skills, and performance to succeed, but they are enhanced when we bask in the light of the right group of allies, coworkers, and colleagues.

Swingset or office building, cubicle or sand box, we are all trying to figure out our place in the world, who our friends are, and what game we're best at—even if the stakes seem higher now than in a game of jacks or tic-tac-toe!

5 Steps for Finding the Right Allies...at the Right Time

Not all allies and cheerleaders are created equal. Some are designed for your personal life, some will be most beneficial during one phase of your career, and some are best for another time period in your personal or professional evolution.

I can vividly recall how perfect timing makes the most of a good ally and completely wastes another. I'm so happy I met some people at one point in my life, and others at a later date, because I simply wasn't in the right place to appreciate all they had to offer in a different time and place. The goal, then, is to find the right ally, for the right position, at the right time, and then engage in such a way that both of you get the most out of this mutually beneficial relationship.

In my many years of networking, relationship-building and ally-finding, I've developed five simple strategies that I feel will help you find the right ally at the right time, for the right position.

1. **Engagement strategy.** Few people feel comfortable walking up to a complete stranger—or someone they hold in high regard—and engaging with them one-on-one. The more similar to an ally or strategic partner you are, the more comfortable with him or her you can be. The first step is to

determine how you can best approach people—
out of the blue, or with an introductory e-mail
or phone call first—and then put that strategy in
place in a real and actionable way.

2. **Vetting strategy.** We start by realizing everybody
has value and something to offer. From there,
we must determine to what extent we'll consider
each person a source, and in what areas. The allies
we want should be positive influences in our lives,
and we want to foster a relationship in which we
can share, learn, and collaborate. For example,
I'm a great person to help you figure out a strategy to reach your goal, so I'm a pretty good source
of information in that regard. However, a physi-
cist I am not, so I would caution you to seriously
qualify any information you might receive from
me on Einstein's theory of relativity. You catego-
rize, mentally, who's good for which subjects or
issues that may arise.

3. **E & E strategizing.** E & E stands for being Effi-
cient and Effective. Remember, a strategy is about
thinking up the back story before writing all the
way to the end. No one likes it when you come
at them with a half-baked plan for which you
haven't thought through the basic details. Even
if I want to help people, if they make it hard for
me, it often falls apart in the engagement phase.
I think most people on the receiving end of that
half-baked plan wonder, "Why should I take time

and dedicate energy to accommodate someone when she hasn't taken the adequate amount of time and energy to help herself?" Make it easy to find allies by having a plan and a strategy in place. If you're going to collaborate with this person, think it through ahead of time: where, when, how long, Skype or phone call, public coffee shop brainstorming sessions once a month, whatever. Think it through before you waste a great opportunity with a perfect ally.

4. **Be a giver, not a taker.** Above all, remember that nobody has "free" time at this stage of the game. If he is someone worth knowing, spending time with, learning from, and benefiting from, he is a busy, busy person. So make it worth his while. Be open to collaboration, and go into any partnership, or mentorship, willing to give as much as you get. You simply have to have an attitude of gratitude if you are to benefit from this mutually beneficial relationship.

5. **Share the catwalk.** Finally, as part of that two-way street, create mutual success in one another's career (and also in your personal relationship with a spouse or significant other). All too often, people take a selfish approach to their careers and even their personal lives. On the surface, it seems to make all the sense in the world: you want to blow your own horn louder than the next person in order to get yourself noticed, advanced, and

onto that coveted next level. After all, in business, the phrases "It's a dog-eat-dog world" and "every man for himself" did not just appear with no context attached to them. But you'll find few partners, let alone allies, wanting to exchange information, favors, introductions, and life lessons when you have that type of attitude. A better strategy for long-term success and satisfaction in work and in life is to share the catwalk, so to speak, and allow those around you to shine as well.

Life Is a Collaboration:
Share the Credit

One thing I've noticed from collaborating with so many people is that you may purposefully have to remind yourself to give as much as you get, at first, but once you start receiving, it becomes easier and easier to give. Considering I've been 29 for many years and I'm not getting any older, perhaps it's a product of my wisdom that I enjoy watching others succeed, and enjoy it even more when I know I've been a part, however small, of that success.

Don't get me wrong: I'm as competitive as the next person—maybe even more so! But that competition is about pushing myself to exceed what I've already accomplished rather than to outperform someone else. I feel joy, pride, wonder, and inspiration when I see friends, colleagues, and mentors achieve a goal I know they've been working long and hard for.

I believe you have to give people credit where credit is due. Why wouldn't I? There's an unlimited amount of praise to go around. It is particularly important when we are working with other folks for a common issue. If you get credit, you've got to pass around the credit. I will accept credit for what I did, and share the praise with my team, saying, "I had the good fortune of working with these folks, and we are all rock stars here." You can't imagine the goodwill and good feelings that kind of credit-sharing can do, for you and your team. And the ripple effect does a couple of things in this instance:

1. **First, it endears people to you.** Folks like it when you don't hog the credit and actually share it around. You're not an innately selfish, narcissistic megalomaniac (because if you were, you might be somewhere pontificating on your own greatness rather than reading this book), so don't be afraid to show people who you really are. Trust me, this is so rare that when you actually do it, people will be amazed.

2. **Second, it enables you to lead and collaborate more effectively because folks know you're not just in it for yourself.** Although there are some professions and lifestyles in which teamwork is not required, most people have to work with

other people to get things done. When doing so, they like to work on a team, *as* a team, not just as a group of anonymous, unrelated people who get to sit by and watch as the "leader" takes all the credit after their hard work. When you do the opposite, when you foster a real team to victory and then share the spoils of that victory, it creates significant buy-in for your people.

3. **Third, it enhances communication immensely.** When people know they can trust you, and that you're not all about you, but about them as well, they will talk to you in a different way. They share more of themselves—and their good work—with you again and again.

I can vividly recall the time when I found myself in a middle management position at the LPGA. There was a point at which I felt I was languishing. I had a ton of ideas and talents outside of the narrow scope of my job and I had no outlet for them. Then I realized that, by building relationships with others and taking on various independent projects, I could maneuver into positions to put that energy to use, and be recognized for my diligence and entrepreneurial spirit, which would ultimately lead to more significant leadership responsibilities.

Look, we all get to that place—in work and in life—where we're kind of just stewing, sitting there marinating in our own juices and basically waiting for something to change. Some of us spend years there and some of us spend a lifetime. But some of us look up after a few days, weeks, or even months in that position and think, "Hey, wait a minute. I'm not going anywhere. There's no easy way out of here. I'm here, and although I may not be able to make a change tomorrow, I'm committed to using my time wisely until I can."

I was able to find that old energy of mine, put it to use, and make what could have been a dead-end position the starting line of a golden opportunity at the LPGA. I had befriended quite a few people during my time there, and some of those relationships proved to be pivotal connections. I believe I mentioned the former LPGA Commissioner Ty Votaw earlier, whose mantra still sticks with me today. Another, whom I count as a very dear friend, is Julie Tyson. After my epiphany about making my current state my best state, Julie and I worked on new strategies to try to create new revenue streams for the organization. We weren't alone. Although putting together revenue-generation and execution strategies was outside of our job descriptions, a group of us were enthusiastic and smart about it, and through our individual expertise, we touched every segment of the organization. Eventually we managed to present the commissioner with a white paper on four different strategies we felt could generate additional revenue. We worked as a team and took the credit for the product as a team. What that gave each of us was an opportunity to develop a direct relationship with the commissioner himself and to show that we each had more value to offer than the narrow scope of our positions. I did not get paid more money for the time, energy, and resources we spent putting that white paper together, but it gave me the opportunity to reposition and re-align myself. I was able to add complexity and depth to my capacity for work and start developing relationships to effectively move around my current situation. Working directly with the LPGA Commissioner and having him view me in another light opened up more doors for me, career-wise.

In every position I've held, I've sought out and collaborated with allies. The same way I ask people questions and read reviews to find the best service providers in town whenever I move to a new city, branch, or location, I would locate the best and brightest, and find a way to talk to them, listen to them, learn from them, share with them, and hopefully work with them.

Along the way I developed a keen understanding that building alliances with the right people is even more important than being recognized for a job well done. Because jobs, departments, contracts, and promotions come and go, but connections—the strong and valuable ones, at least—last a lifetime.

The Power of Participation:
Collaborating for Maximum Effectiveness

So often in life we simply go through the motions. If we're lucky, we recognize that life isn't about solitary pursuits, but intended to be lived in partnership and collaboration with others. Particularly in the workplace, whether it's a corporate setting or your own start-up, learning from that playground mentality how to play well with others is an invaluable tool for maximizing the daily collaborations that are the fuel of any business success.

Success is more than simply being recognized for your talents and abilities—it's also about knowing where to put your dividends to get the maximum return. Just as financial experts talk about the importance of spreading around your monetary investments, this sage advice can be put into practice in the workplace as well. By consistently investing in and acknowledging the contributions of others as well as fostering the lasting relationships that doing so can build, you can earn the loyalty and the respect of those around you. You can be recognized as a leader, a team builder, and someone who is willing to share the spotlight. The positivity and the influence that such an attitude brings with it is invaluable when it comes to accomplishing great things—something that's sadly lost on many professionals (men and women alike) in the current marketplace.

The road to success in your career and your relationships is about pushing yourself to perform better instead of simply jockeying for the spotlight—often at the expense of valuable team members who can do more harm than good for your career when they learn you're a credit-hog instead of a credit-sharer. It's about participation. It's about going to work every day with the spirit of sharing and caring about the people on your team. I know it isn't always easy, but I also know there is always something valuable to be learned from every member of your team, even if it's just how *not* to behave in a social or workplace setting! But more than what *not* to do, there is so much to learn about what *to* do, as a manager, a leader, a coworker, a colleague, or a team member. This active sense of participation involves overcoming the fear of meeting new people and learning how to interact with them. Then, it is about becoming good at identifying the types of individuals who can provide support (as opposed to those who will question or be negative) and objectivity to tell you the truth (as opposed to those who just tell you what you think you want to hear).

We all need to be confident in our skill sets, and act accordingly, but recognizing and addressing our imperfections is a strength, not a weakness. Too many people blindly move forward without ever pausing to listen to those trusted mentors, friends, coworkers, and allies who are willing to tap them on the shoulder and say, "Hey, can I offer you some constructive criticism?" Whether you ultimately act on it, hearing it, listening to it, and vetting it appropriately is real strength. Part of vetting the information is considering the source. For example, everyone has their own unique orientation, set of biases, and motivations. If you get to know what they are you will be able to engage the right people at the right time along your learning curve to get the support, information, and resources you need to reach peak performance or connect with your passion.

Meet *Julie Tyson*

Meet my friend, confidante, mentor, colleague, and ally, Julie Tyson. Julie is someone I befriended when I worked at the LPGA (and one of my co-conspirators in the white paper for the Commissioner). She is currently the Vice President of Business Development at the PGA Tour.

She is one of the best people I know at reading people and figuring out how to engage them accordingly, so I thought she'd be the perfect person with whom to discuss tips on collaboration and ally-finding.

Julie is a salesperson by training, and that is what she does day in and day out. She is really quite extraordinary. One of the things I find fascinating about Julie is that she engages with people in her personal and professional life in much the same way, and seems to approach most people with not only an open mind, but also a genuine interest in what makes them tick. Her first step, Julie says, is fairly obvious. "Just get to know the other person," she explains. "Go kind of slow and understand, first, where is their starting point? Whether it's personal or professional, where is their starting point for their discussion with you? So as best as you can, try to get to know a little about their background and their experience, and from that, what you'll start to see is where their biases lie, kind of where their strong opinions sit."

Patience is a big part of Julie's process for networking and collaboration as well. "Part of this," she explains, "is going in sort of slowly because you're asking them to make an investment in you, whether that's with their time or some sort of reputational risk. So, you're asking them to make an investment, and they want to know what you're all about and whether or not they can trust you. So you have to take some time, let that evolve naturally."

But more than patience, Julie relies on intuition and acute listening skills to find that one thing a person really cares about, and then learning how to share it with them. She explains, "Every person on the planet has insecurities—everyone. And I try to get people talking and I try to make them feel comfortable enough, that somewhere along the way that they will reveal what their insecurities are. If you can disarm that insecurity, you get yourself to a place where you can have a much more productive and honest conversation."

But Julie cautions that it's not about being mercenary or manipulative, but simply disarming the other person so you can start with a blank slate based on trust, not fear. "Because otherwise," she warns, "if that insecurity is present, it will be in front of the two of you always. And that's where defense mechanisms come in. So, the faster you can try to figure out what those insecurities are and disarm them so that they feel like they can trust you, then you get to a more honest place in the discussion and you can actually just deal with the issue, not with all the other stuff that sits out there."

Asking questions—and actually listening to how the other person answers—is another big part of Julie's success in engaging with people. "I try to ask a lot of questions," she says. "There are a handful of things that are important to people. Spend time figuring out what matters to them. So, usually, talking about someone's family, talking about their kids, talking about where they grew up, and talking about an accomplishment that they are really happy about."

Not only does Julie ask questions of the other person, but while communicating, she's also asking them of herself: "I just start to look at, what are the things that they like? What are the things that irritate them? How do they interact with other people in the room? What's their body language? And you're kind of just poking around just to see. And some of it is prodding and some of it is really genuinely listening."

Most of all, Julie explains, it's not about tips, strategies, or tactics, or tricks of the trade, but about sincere and honest relationship-building. She states emphatically, "I think it starts from a place of honestly caring about people. I really genuinely care about people. I am interested in them and I think everybody has something interesting to share." When others see and respond to that interest, Julie says, insecurities fade and a genuine sense of trust can form. "Trust issues are the thing that accelerate or decelerate the speed with which you can disarm someone," is her motto.

Julie is also quick to point out that positive influencers are to be sought out and appreciated more than those who might sap or drain our energies and take rather than give or collaborate. "I tend to naturally gravitate to people who are extremely competent, in whatever their field is, and who worked very hard at it, and who, generally, are passionate," she explains. "Because from that, they're generally more positive people, so they're better to be around. They don't make excuses often, and I am not a big fan of excuses. It's like, you either do the job or you don't, and sometimes bad things happen and you pick up and you move on when that happens."

Julie is also attracted to a certain type of person: "I look for people who are committed to self-improvement, in some way, shape, or form. I gravitate to people who want to always grow, like that's a life-long thing."

Julie confesses she can be a little *too* interested in other people, to the point of missing opportunities or perhaps not sharing as much as she might about herself to those she is "interrogating." She fondly recalls one of her best interviews: "I was the one being interviewed, but I didn't impart one single thing about myself in the entire time we were in the interview. It wasn't on purpose, I just kept asking questions because I was honestly curious about this person's viewpoints, what they cared about. I walked out of the interview and I thought I bombed it. I thought, 'Oh my gosh, how am I gonna get a job where I didn't tell anybody anything about myself?' And the feedback on that interview was that I was by far and away the best candidate that person had ever interviewed. And I don't know what that says about human beings but I think for the most part, people want to be around people who make them feel good about themselves."

When it comes to improving your people skills, it's probably no surprise that Julie recommends spending time with other people. "If you want to learn," she suggests, "spend some time around someone who is really good at generating a rapport with people because you'll see that they genuinely like people and care about them. That's the starting point. But from there, there's a lot of warmth that they generate very quickly, and people feel trusting. They trust that person. You really do have to earn people's trust, and my tactic to do that is to just make them feel safe and comfortable, like they're enjoying themselves, because those are three kind of basic needs: joy, comfort, and safety. So, that's kind of where I start, because that is what works for me."

Like myself, Julie has a strong passion for making alliances, and allies in general. "They are the most important thing," she explains, and for a variety of reasons. "For one thing, from a career perspective, nobody ever goes it alone. You can be the smartest person, but if you can't get a deal done, you can't get promoted—nobody ever does it alone. Everyone needs an advocate. The most important thing you can do in your career is to truly, genuinely develop trusted relationships with people from all parts of not only your organization, but the industry as well. No one's going to pull a trigger for someone they don't trust, and they're going to do their homework on you. Those allies come in real handy because they're going to go to battle for you and say, 'She's great to deal with. She will deliver everything she says and more. She has tremendous character,' or whatever. Allies are the most important thing you can have, bar none."

Julie cautions not to pre-judge who might be the best or worst allies based on rank, title, or position alone. "Allies come in all shapes and sizes," she warns. "Allies don't just have to be at the top of an organization. There are lots of opinion leaders that sit [at various levels] in an organization that can make or break you. And no one is more important than another." Julie is also quick to point out that oftentimes it is the most common face you see that can do the most good for you and your career, such as an assistant, secretary, intern, or other key support person who doesn't only know what he knows, but what everyone else knows as well! One of the most strategic alliances you can make at work is with that person in a "gatekeeper" role, that one ally who may not be seated at the top, but has his or her finger on the pulse of how to get you there.

When Julie and I worked at the LPGA together, for example, the assistant to the commissioner was a very important person to ally ourselves with because that was a gatekeeper who can allow or prevent access. And in organizations, access is the first step to alliance. Gatekeepers become especially strong allies when they can provide a timely tip or a warning about an impending meeting or interview. Recalls Julie, "Maybe Corporate is going to come and ask you a question about something. The gatekeeper can give you a heads up and say, 'You should be prepared for this.' So that way you're always putting your best foot forward."

Alliances don't just go up, but sideways and even down as well. As Julie points out, "I think that goes hand-in-hand with recognizing that everyone has value. And not just trying to manage up, but also, laterally, down, that sort of thing. Just being a decent human being."

One of the challenges Julie notes about forging alliances is the difference between quantity and quality. In other words, it's not about how many people you know, but the quality of the people you align yourself with. The fact is, some people aren't good allies because of one reason or another. Perhaps they're selfish, perhaps they're arrogant, and sometimes they're flat-out incompetent. "If they're incompetent,"

Julie explains, "I always look at them as a short-term issue because at a certain point, they're not going to continue in that role because naturally someone more competent will slide into their spot. That's just the law of how it all works out. If they're competent and they're irritating to me, then the problem is mine to solve. So, if they're good at their jobs and I just don't seem to have anything in common with them, then I have to work harder again, going back to, what's the insecurity and why are we not finding common ground? That's on me."

This brings us to the point of self-assessment, and realizing that sometimes we're the weakest link in an alliance, and may have to work on some of those "weaknesses" to play a little better with others. Julie cautions, "That's where the emotional IQ has to catch up to the intellectual IQ for you to be able to navigate. You're always going to have difficult people, and if I was still really employing my skillsets and thinking, 'Okay, I have to manage that insecurity of his or hers,' then I would figure out a way to manage around that." I think we can all relate to that emotional trigger that sends our well-laid plans right into the stratosphere, and our hopes and dreams crashing right back to earth. But as adults, we have to find a way around, under, over, or sometimes right through our obstacles, and that often results in compromise in the workplace. In the case of an emotional trigger, such as condescending male colleagues, Julie recommends proceeding with caution. "You have to back away from it. You have to take a big deep breath and think to yourself, 'Okay, what part of my ego or my insecurity do I have to make subservient to make this work? Because it's obviously not a functional thing in this room. It's not going to work for me.' And it's not like you have to cater to people or kowtow or swallow your pride or behave in a less-than-who-you are way. It's more about thinking, 'Okay, well, clearly, there's something I'm not doing properly. And if the guy or girl is really competent and really has some issues and you're unable to navigate them, cut your losses, move on. Start over with somebody else. But for the most part, if you're able to suppress the emotion in those discussions and simply clue in to the benefits of managing insecurity, figuring out their biases, getting to know them, and letting them get to know you, eventually, you'll always get there. Eventually. Some people just take more time."

Clearly, Julie has taken the time, the energy, and the compromise to forge long-lasting alliances that have propelled her straight to the top!

Parting Words

I hope you enjoyed Julie's words of wisdom and learned, as I did, from her masterful alliance-making! Over and above that, I hope the steps I've shared with you in this section have helped convince you that making allies is one of the most critical things you can do to accelerate and propel your dreams forward, whatever they may be.

No one does it alone, and the sooner you acknowledge and accept that fact, the sooner you can embrace the power and passion of those with whom you come into contact every day. For they are the ones who can help guide, challenge, and propel your passion and purpose forward, if only you'll let them by learning to play well with others, on and off the playground!

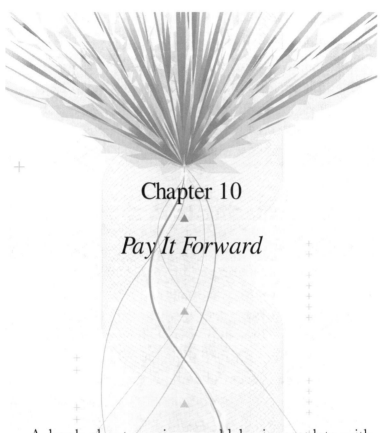

Chapter 10

Pay It Forward

A book about passion would be incomplete without a discussion about the importance of sharing that
passion with the rest of the world. And I do mean *the
world.* Whether that world means around your home,
around your corner, around your workplace, or around
the globe, you can't keep all this good stuff to yourself!
Look at me: if someone had told me a few years ago that
I would be writing a book to share with folks all over the
world or that I would establish a professional development program to help broaden my mentoring reach, I would

have laughed and looked at the calendar to confirm it was April Fool's Day!

But as I've lived my life, as I've succeeded and failed, lived and learned, done and failed to do and done again, I've realized that the true purpose of all of our lives is not just to play well with others, as we just read about in Chapter 9, but also to share well with others.

Sharing Is Caring

I am convinced that I am where I am today because of the caring and sharing of others on this planet. From former professors to classmates, bosses to coworkers, friends to mentors to allies, I have benefitted from dozens of close relationships that helped propel me to a higher plane, be it professionally or personally. I believe I would still be successful without their help, but not to this degree.

We all owe a debt of gratitude to those known and unknown trailblazers, allies, mentors, family members, and friends who have allowed us to stand on their shoulders, either for a better view of the landscape ahead or for a boost up and over a significant challenge, road block, or detour. But words are cheap. It's easy enough to say "thank you" and move on, but harder still to do something physical, concrete, and beneficial to *show* our gratitude rather than just tell it.

That's why I tell anyone who will listen, "Sharing is caring." We have to care enough to share what we've learned, to help others learn the lessons that came so hard to us, so that they don't have to reinvent the wheel.

Anything else is a hollow victory, from my vantage point.

Paying It Forward

There are many ways we can share our success with those around us. We can bring our team along for the ride, we can hire those whom we know can do the very best job, or who simply need a job. We can be a powerful force in the lives of others through the simple concept of paying it forward.

The concept of paying it forward began as a novel by Catherine Ryan Hyde and later became a movie starring Kevin Spacey and Helen Hunt. Both projects helped introduce the world to the simple concept of doing a good deed for someone and asking them, in turn, to do a good deed for someone else. In such a way, we can affect the entire world with a simple, random act of kindness.

It's easy in this big world, in the face of natural disasters, financial collapse, government shutdowns, and plain old bad news, to feel powerless. But with the concept of paying it forward, everyone can make a difference, and the more people who try, the bigger a difference can be made. What I like about paying it forward is that it's active. It's an action plan, really. So many lessons are just in your head; paying it forward is out in the world. You reach out, you do for another, and, in turn, they do the same. Like a chain reaction, one act turns into a dozen acts, a hundred, a hundred thousand...maybe more.

That was my goal in founding TheSpark. I receive more than my fair share of requests to mentor young to mid-level professionals and law students. Most know what they want their career, image, and lifestyle to look like. They also know that they have to go after it or they'll never achieve it. The problem is that they don't know *how* to achieve it. I'm happy to help them with candid, unbiased advice, but my challenge is always carving out time to do so for all the people who are asking for help. So I established TheSpark (*www.thesparkhq.com*) to broaden my reach. With it, I talk to larger groups of people by video and conference calls to answer their questions and offer strategies and techniques to help shorten learning curves. It's not the unlimited, one-on-one mentoring you traditionally see, but via TheSpark, I'm able to pay the help I received forward.

My goal for you, in writing this book, is also to pay it forward. I took the first step by writing all this down, sharing it with you, giving you the tools you need to embrace your passion, make a change, and reinvigorate or simply reboot your life plans or goals and succeed at a higher level. In short, I've sparked your passion. Now it's your turn: I want you to take your own passion-sparking experience and use it to engage others to spark their own passion, creating the momentum, or forward movement in life for mutual success and benefit.

7 Ways to Pay It Forward

Before I conclude my portion of this chapter and hand you over to my good friend and colleague, Keith Wyche, I want to leave you with seven simple ways you can pay it forward, right now, today, with no waiting.

1. **Start small.** The beauty of paying it forward is that it only takes one act to start a chain reaction that could truly span the globe. It can be anything: helping a friend fill out a job resume, letting someone know of an opening in your company, or guiding a job seeker to a great professional resource, club, or organization. People are starving for help, and all they need is a crumb to get started.

2. **Random is great, focused is better.** I tend to pay it forward where I'll do the most benefit, which typically involves providing opportunities and learning for the folks I come in contact with on a daily basis. An open door here, a kind word there, and soon you're doing real good for real people whom you can watch grow and evolve all around you.

3. **Plan ahead.** Most people think that paying it forward is all about the random, opportune moments

that present themselves in a day, but it can also be the good you do in a more focused, strategic, and calculated way. For instance, you can create a letter of recommendation template that you can fill out, quickly and simply, for those who might benefit from your support. Don't neglect the opportunity to open the door for a random stranger, but don't let other, more purposeful acts of kindness slip through your fingers because you're unprepared.

4. **Rinse, lather, repeat.** Paying it forward isn't a holiday, special event, or one-time thing. For me, and for many of my colleagues and allies, it's a daily event. There are so many opportunities to help people, you'll be amazed if you just try it once. And if you try it once, you won't be able to stop. Seeing someone benefit from an act of kindness doesn't just change their world, it changes yours as well.

5. **The gift that keeps on giving.** Paying it forward really is a gift, and that's how I often treat it. For birthdays, Christmas, and other card-giving holidays I'll always write a little note in the card that says, "In honor of this special occasion, I donated a set of encyclopedias to the local Boy's Club," or something of that nature. It's never their only gift, but it's always a part of the way I give to others, and give back to my many friends and allies.

It's also a great reminder for them to pay it forward in *their* next gift!

6. **Make it a habit.** The best way to pay it forward regularly is simply to...pay it forward regularly. It really is just as simple, and as complicated, as that. The more you pay it forward, the more you will want to pay it forward. Doing good makes you feel good, there's no doubt about it. But more than that, it makes others feel good, and that is a feeling that is truly contagious.

7. **Trust others to do the same.** The problem of (and the opportunity in) paying it forward is that you must rely on others to keep the chain going, to not break the chain and let everyone else down. Unfortunately, you can't control how others behave, so you have to trust others to do unto others. And that can be the hardest challenge of all. One way to counteract a broken link in the "pay it forward" chain is simply to redouble your efforts and pay it forward twice!

As you can see, it's easier than you may have thought to put your words to work and make the world a better place, starting right now. And now, before we go, I'd like to introduce you to someone I think will double the message of paying it forward.

Meet *Keith Wyche*

Keith Wyche is the former president of Cub Foods and is now the CEO of ACME Markets, a SUPERVALU company. He is one of the highest-ranking African American executives in the United States and the author of *Corner Office Rules: The 10 Realities of Executive Life* (Kandelle Enterprises, 2013). Despite his lofty title and vast number of accomplishments, Keith did not come from a pedigree of corporate executives. Instead, he worked his way up through the chain. I spoke to Keith about this concept because it is important to hold the door open for the people following behind us. In short, Keith is a great example of paying it forward, again and again. He is willing to share what he has learned with other executives trying to reach the top of the ladder. For my money, Keith's story provides a great example of this concept and is a great way to end the book.

Keith's story—that is his *success* story—begins with someone else paying it forward for him. "I was coming out of college," he explains. "I had just graduated, I was 21, and AT&T was hiring sales reps, but I was considered young because I hadn't been a professional salesperson. But there was this lady, Ernestine Turner was her name, and she was a recruiter, and she said, 'There's something about you...I can't guarantee you'll make it, but I'm gonna give you the opportunity to go into this program.' And it was a program where basically, if you didn't make it through the training period, you got fired." Keith recalls, "It was a very intensive situation. And for me, that showed me that there are people in this world that will give you an opportunity, when on the surface, you almost don't deserve one."

Keith has never forgotten the lesson Ernestine Turner taught him about paying it forward, and provides some simple steps for helping others help themselves. "First," he points out, "you have to be prepared for when the opportunity arises, but second, look for those people who can help you up. And what I have found, you can call it destiny, you can call it God's favor, but there have always been people in my life who, when I was willing to step out of fear and try something or do something, who would give me that opportunity, who would open that door." Keith notes that you can give, or receive, the gift of paying it forward at anytime, anywhere, from anyone. "They didn't all look like me," he points out. "They were different races, genders, creeds, what have you, but there were always people there."

Keith also points to what he calls "Encouragers," folks who pay it forward in little ways all day long. "I've always surrounded myself with encouragers," he explains, "people who would help me up and hold me up when I didn't feel like holding myself up. And that was very important, because I came of age, corporate-wise, in the early '80s, when there were not a lot of people of color in any leadership positions, and many of the few that were there, were just so glad to be there, and so protective of their space, that they had a kind of 'There can only be one of us' mentality."

The sound of gratitude runs through everything Keith told me about his past—and his future. He says he learned at that early age to reinvest that gratitude by joining powerful organizations where he could be helped, and help others. "I joined National Black MBA in 1984, when I was 24 years old, and the National Conference of Christians and Jews, and there were always people and organizations that opened their arms to me to say, 'If you're willing, we'll give you a shot.'"

When I first approached Keith about being interviewed for this book, the first thing he said to me was, "How can I help you? How can I be a resource?" So I know firsthand that the man is interested, invested, and involved in paying it forward, 100-percent of the time. And these aren't just random events; Keith has a specific philosophy in mind when he reaches out to help someone else up. "My philosophy on paying it forward," he says, "is that there is always someone coming from behind, right? There's always someone who is trying to go where you are. And so, even as far back as high school, I was always looking for that. When I was a sophomore, I was looking for the freshman who came in bright-eyed and bushy-tailed and I would say to him, 'Hey, kid, let me show you where the locker's at, let me show...,' because I've always thought there was something you can learn and share to that next generation; we should always share life lessons."

Keith's philosophy isn't just a happy accident, but a very powerful—and purposeful—belief. He explains, "I believe in living life on purpose. I think we were all put here for a purpose. And sometimes those lessons learned are from mistakes too, right? They're not always the things that we do well, so sharing those lessons is important."

Keith adds that even though he's old-school, he's embraced the social media age to pay it forward online. He explains, "One of the things that I love about this social media age is that instead of having a one-to-one audience or speaking in front of 50 folks, you can get on LinkedIn and share your messages. You can tweet. So most of my coaching and mentoring and those things right now are actually done via social networking." In addition to mentoring online, Keith is a big believer in what he calls "organizational mentoring," or belonging to groups where he can be assured of giving the most in a concentrated and concerted way. "I'm still very much involved with the Black MBA, NSN, and Executive 50," he says. "Again, it's not one-to-one mentoring and coaching but it's kind of organizational in nature that I can maybe share a podcast."

Even Keith's book, *Corner Office Rules*, was another way of paying it forward. "The biggest motivation I have for writing a book," he says, "was because people kept coming to me over and over and over again, to be their coach, to be their mentor. So I said, 'Let me just write now what little I know, and so at least package that, so they get that.' And if they have questions for me on that, we can have a talk."

Keith concludes that his philosophy of paying it forward is more than just a passing phase, but a lifestyle. "We have to prepare this next generation of leadership," he insists. "And so, to me, true leadership creates future leaders, and we should never be so big and so high and so mighty that we don't reach back and pull somebody else up."

As always, Keith backs up his words with a proven commitment to paying it forward in his daily life, taking time out of his busy schedule as a motivational speaker and best-selling author to help this new author out! For more insights from Keith's blog, visit him at *www.keithwyche .com*.

Parting Words

Remember, there *is* no finish line; life is all about the journey—where you go, how you get there, what you experience, learn, and value, and, in particular, whom you meet along the way.

To spend one's life in pursuit of a single, mindless goal, to win at all costs no matter who you hurt to get to the top, will only leave you standing alone, with no friends or allies to share that victory with.

I am not a missionary. I am here to win, to succeed, and to reach a series of goals I still have yet to accomplish. But that doesn't mean I can't help others along the way. We all can. Success at all costs, or to the exclusion of all relationships, is an empty victory indeed. Share the wealth, spread it around, and you'll find that every victory you celebrate—whether it's yours or one of your allies'—is an even more joyous event than you could have imagined.

For me, the only way to spend Life at the Speed of Passion is to spend it in the company of good friends, close family, great allies, and a host of high achievers who help me help them, and vice versa.

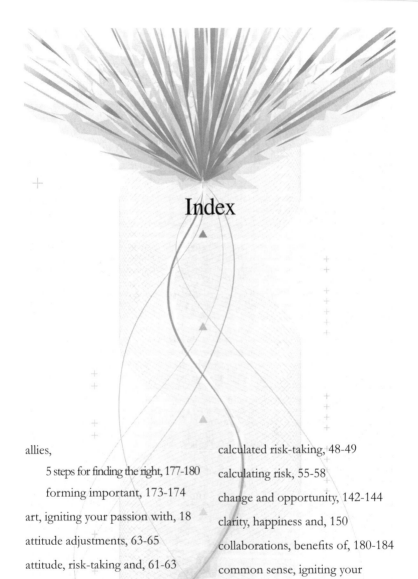

Index

About the Author

Eve Wright: *Calculated Risk-Taker*

Eve Wright has never been the kind of woman to wait for opportunities—in business or in her personal life. This big-picture-thinking, calculated-risk-taking executive learned the hard way that, for her goals, she would have to create opportunities rather than wait for them. It's a philosophy that's steered Wright's successful career in one of the most male-dominated industries in the world—professional sports—as well as in entrepreneurship and authorship.

Wright serves as a board director for USA Track & Field and hadn't even reached 35 when she earned a top spot as Vice President and Associate General Counsel for the Miami HEAT and the AmericanAirlines Arena. Additionally, she and her husband own and operate US Bulldog Security Bars, which manufactures and distributes theBulldog Bar home security device.

Her track record of success ranges from the corporate law firm setting to the Ladies Professional Golf Association (LPGA) to the Member Team of the National Basketball Association. She is a relatively young executive who's enjoyed a meteoric rise through the ranks of Corporate America and the professional sports world.

Wright's message has captivated audiences large and small (male and female), at forums that have ranged from colleges to the Super Bowl. She has been featured in various publications, including the *Sports Business Journal*, *Black Enterprise*, *Success Magazine*, *Legacy Magazine*, *African-American Golfer's Digest*, the *Atlanta Tribune*, the *Atlanta Post, and The DePauw* magazines, to name a few. She's also been featured on *Fox Business News*, *BetterTV*, and The Golf Channel television network.

Ms. Wright has received several awards, among them the coveted *Sports Business Journal's* Forty Under 40 Award, *Black Enterprise Magazine's* 40 Under 40, The Thurgood Marshall Fund Distinguished Young Leader

Award, Executive 50 Award, and the National Bar Association's 40 Under 40 Nation's Best Advocates.

Ms. Wright is a graduate of DePauw University, where she received a Bachelor of Arts in Economics and International Business. She earned her Doctor of Jurisprudence from Indiana University School of Law. She resides with her husband, Dr. Ken Taylor, and daughter.